Praise for
The Questioning God

Ant Greenham presents an intriguing analysis of the world's monotheistic religions and their view of God, through the lens of how God is perceived to relate to the questions of human beings. Using broad strokes, he paints a generalized picture of this situation. In essence, he argues that Islam suppresses the questioning of God through its focus on submission to the will of Allah. On the opposite end of the spectrum, Greenham presents the Jewish faith as being so open to questioning God that this questioning has undermined an ultimate certainty in God. This leaves the Christian faith, which Greenham examines in both its Roman Catholic and Evangelical forms. While Vatican II opened the Roman Catholic Church to a more positive view of questioning, it has left certain theological positions too sacrosanct to be questioned. Evangelicals, in the meantime, have become too closed to the questioning of authority (both political and religious) and Greenham outlines some of the potential dangers inherent in this lack of questioning.

(Dr. Danielson's full review is available on our web site at http://energion.net/2012/02/book-review-the-questioning-god)

Robert Danielson
Faculty Associate
Asbury Theological Seminary
Wilmore, Kentucky

Dr. Greenham has successfully merged scholarship and faith, challenging his readers not to fear inquiry but to embrace it. Ant brings us a means of confidently engaging our questioning God while providing us with an effective means of sharing our faith among those of the major monotheistic religions using the interrogative approach. A thought-provoking read!

Robert McKibben
Pastor, Daphne United Methodist Church
Alabama

There is little in life so scintillating as a brief book with pungent, exciting, thought-provoking content. Ant Greenham in *The Questioning God* has achieved that goal with remarkable succinctness. For example, I learned more about Islam in chapters 3 and 4 than in all the rest of my reading on the subject in the last five years. Don't miss this prescient monograph.

Paige Patterson
President, Southwestern Baptist Theological Seminary
Ft. Worth, TX

This enjoyable book is one of a kind. It deals with one of the most critical issues in relating to Muslims. Lessons from Jewish and Muslim traditions in light of the style of Jesus are drawn and presented to us in a very practical and helpful fashion.

Georges Houssney
Director, Horizons International

Dr. Greenham offers a brief, but refreshing and provocative introduction to the importance of asking questions regarding one's religious beliefs. Such questions, he persuasively argues, lack any accusatory tone towards God; rather they seek clarification regarding human beliefs about God. Greenham argues for an intellectual honesty in the matter of auditing one's beliefs precisely because humanity's cognitive limitations require questions in order to assure beliefs about God correspond to the Truth. The content successfully strikes a commendable balance between naïve realism and utter skepticism providing a healthy approach to establishing sufficient justification for beliefs one holds about God.

Bruce A. Little
Professor of Philosophy
Director of the L. Russ Bush Center for Faith and Culture
Southeastern Baptist Theological Seminary
Wake Forest, North Carolina

The Questioning God
An Inquiry for Muslims, Jews, and Christians

Ant Greenham

Energion Publications
P. O. Box 841
Gonzalez, FL 32560

www.energionpubs.com

2012

Cover Design: Jason Neufeld (jasonneufelddesign.com)

ISBN10: 1-893729-19-2
ISBN13: 978-1-893729-19-3

Library of Congress Control Number: 2012934349

Energion Publications
P. O. Box 841
Gonzalez, FL 32560

To the Questioning God,
with gratitude—not least for the gift
of my questioning wife,
Eva.

Table of Contents

From the Editors

The Areopagus is a hill in Athens that was once the meeting place of a Greek council. Paul preached on that hill while visiting Athens, presenting the gospel to the Athenian council and converting one of them (Acts 17). It thus provides an excellent name for this series of booklets that examines important issues in understanding Christian beliefs and developing sound Christian practice. Each booklet is intentionally short – less than 80 pages in length – and provides an academically sound and biblically rooted examination of a particular question about doctrine or practice or an area of basic Christian belief.

The Areopagus series is orthodox in doctrine but not bound to the doctrinal statements of any denomination. It is both firm in conviction and irenic in tone. Authors have been chosen for their ability to understand a topic in depth and present it clearly.

Each book is rigorous in scholarship because we believe the church deserves no less. Yet the volumes are accessible in style as we also believe that there are many pastors and laypersons in the church who desire to think deeply and critically about the issues that confront the church today in its life and mission in the world.

In keeping with these convictions, the authors in this series are either professors who are also actively involved in ministry, pastors who have not only thought through the issues but whose ministry has been guided by their convictions, or laypersons whose faith and commitment to the lordship of Jesus Christ and his church have contributed to the Great Commission Jesus gave to all of his followers (Matt. 28:18-20).

The *Areopagus Critical Christian Issues* series is not only meant to help the church think differently. We hope that those who read its volumes will be different, for the gospel is about the transformation of the whole person – mind, heart, and soul.

We take the words of the apostle Paul seriously when he says to the Athenians that God "has fixed a day on which he will have the world judged in righteousness by a man whom he has appointed; and of this he has given assurance to all by raising him from the dead" (Acts 17:31).

Allan R. Bevere
David Alan Black
Editors

Introduction

A questioning approach lies at the heart of our relationship with God. That's how he engages us. In fact, questioning (or free inquiry) is central to our being human. Yet the major monotheistic religions vary markedly on this matter. Islam, in its essence, requires submission. Unfortunately, this is fatal to free inquiry. Muslims are not self-critical, especially when Islam itself is questioned. Yet Muslims must be engaged with questions. They are no less human than anyone else.

In contrast to Islam, Judaism is characterized by intense questioning. Jews are adept at challenging all things Jewish, including policies of the State of Israel. This has strengths and weaknesses. Self-criticism is strong, but answers are elusive. In particular, Jews avoid questions on the claims of Christ. Yet engaging the Jewish messiah is imperative.

Finally, Christians argue rightly for unassailable truth, especially when preaching the gospel. However, the spirit of free inquiry is often lost in the name of piety. When Christians exhibit a spirit of unthinking submission, this dehumanizes us and hinders our witness to the questioning God. Instead, we need biblical questioning. This means two things: I must come to know the *questioning* God. Then, as he engages me as a questioning being, I should treat *you* as a questioning being.

I hope this short book gives Christians a way to evaluate the major monotheistic systems, including our own. If, in the process, we learn to think and act differently—as the questioning God would require—I will be grateful.

I have one caveat. Due to length constraints, my comparison of the three major monotheisms is selective. I concentrate on questioning. Even within these confines, others writing on monotheistic inquiry would include details I left out. Also, many would say a lot more about each tradition as such. However, despite my brevity, I have tried to avoid any unfair representation in the pages which follow. Whether I have succeeded is for the questioning reader to determine.

1

The Bible's Questioning God

At first glance, it seems the Bible's earliest question is put to Eve by the Serpent in the Garden of Eden. Enticingly, he asks her, "Did God actually say, 'You shall not eat of any tree in the garden?'" (Gen 3:1). It is a foundational question, since it has led to the sorry saga of fallen humanity. But that's not where questioning in the Bible begins.

Before our first parents doubted God's word, ate the fruit of the tree of the knowledge of good and evil, and died spiritually, another question was repeatedly on Adam's mind. It was something like "What's its name?" This query emerged from his need of a companion. As it turned out, God provided Adam's soul mate in his special creation of Eve. But before doing so, perhaps to enhance the introduction of his wife, God required him to examine one non-human creature after another, and then name each one (Gen 2:19). Adam must have exercised inquiry here. God didn't provide the names; Adam had to come up with them. And in all likelihood, Adam's thought about each name included questions of the creature's suitability for him.

Finally though, after God's intervention, he had to answer the "What's *her* name?" question and did so with delight (Gen 2:23). Unlike the lesser creatures, she was one just like him. In fact, Eve was no less made in God's image than he was, as Genesis 1:27 affirms: Male and female are *both* made in God's image. Moreover, since men and women both have dominion over the rest of creation (Gen 1:28), we may infer the inquiry God expected of Adam when it came to his environment, applied to Eve. In other words, people bearing God's image had to figure things out right at the very beginning, even before the fall. This is how the human story begins.

Our foundational identity as human beings, female and male, is inextricably linked to questioning, to inquiry. The fall of humanity notwithstanding, people are repeatedly called to respond to God in the context of mental and spiritual engagement. And the centrality of a questioning approach is reflected throughout the Bible.

Consider the following incidents: God asks Adam and Eve, "Where are you? . . . Have you eaten of the tree? . . . What is this you have done?" (Gen 3:9-13). God challenges Abraham: "Number the stars, if you are able to number them" (Gen 15:5). At the burning bush, following several of Moses' questions and God's answers, God asks: "What is that in your hand? . . . Who has made man's mouth?" (Ex 4:2-11). Or, at the same place (Horeb), another time, God asks (twice), "What are you doing here, Elijah?" (1 Kings 19:9 & 13). Job questions God and then God asks Job, "Who is this that darkens counsel by words without knowledge?" (Job 38:2). Despite the devastating magnificence of his appearance to Isaiah, God asks, "Whom shall I send, and who will go for us?" (Isa 6:8). He also asks Jeremiah, "What do you see?" (Jer 1:11), and Ezekiel (and by extension, Israel), "What do you mean by repeating this proverb?" (Ezek 18:2). It is evident God expects engagement.

As we move to the New Testament, Jesus does the same. Concerning John the Baptist he asks, "What did you go out into the wilderness to see?" (Matt 11:7). He asks the rich young man, "Why do you ask me about what is good?" (Matt 19:17). He asks two blind men, "What do you want me to do for you?" (Matt 20:32). Discussing the payment of tax to Caesar, he asks, "Whose likeness and inscription is this?" (Matt 22:20). Considering divorce he asks, "What did Moses command you?" (Mark 10:3). And crucially, he asks the now-seeing man born blind a question we all have to answer, "Do you believe in the Son of Man?" (John 9:35), or as he puts it to his disciples, "Who do you say that I am?" (Matt 16:15). The God-Man (Jesus) expects engagement too.

It should be clear from this brief selection of divine questions that God not only expects engagement but engagement with himself. Space doesn't allow an exegesis of each question, but in every case the focus is on encounter with God and his ways.

This encountering focus is also found in God's outright commands. God isn't limited to questions! But whatever way God directs his word to us, the overarching purpose is the same—that sinful human beings enter into and be nourished in a living relationship with him. In fact, God's basic desire (and covenant promise) may best be expressed in the sentence, "I will be their God and they will be my people." It is found in numerous places, in both Testaments.[1] However, as individuals turn to God and become his people, we are always mentally and spiritually engaged. It is not a case of blind acceptance.

God asks questions of us to elicit our response, and we may even question him in return. Our questions may point in many different directions though. We thus turn now to our identity as inquirers and to the nature of our questions.

---

1   Passages include (but are by no means limited to) Exod 6:7, Deut 29:13, 2 Sam 7:24, Jer 24:7 and 31:33, Ezek 36:28 and 37:27, 2 Cor 6:16, 1 Pet 2:9–10, and Rev 21:3.

2
What It Means to be Human

Since the questioning God made people in his image, human beings ask questions. Udo Middelmann asserts that we "are the only beings who are not satisfied with merely living instinctually. . . . We do not just accept things but wonder why. . . . We think and act in the bounds of moral and philosophical categories. . . . While animals respond from instinct, we learn to question" (Middelmann, 126). Vishal Mangalwadi spells out this difference in an example from India. He asks audiences what they do first on returning home in the dark. Typically, they flip a switch, light a candle, or find some way to illuminate the dwelling. In contrast, a dog entering a dark house finds its bed and lies down. People do this, too, if the power is out or they have no matches. However, they work to resolve the illumination problem, if it continues, as soon as possible. The reason for the difference "is that we make light because, while we are made in the image of the Creator who made light, our dog is not. Animals are not creative in the sense that they do not create culture and history" (Mangalwadi, 261).[2] Such creating is what people do.

Creating culture, which includes finding ways to light a house, is a matter of searching and questioning. Philip Jenkins argues, "We should acknowledge the divinely inspired inquisitiveness and creativity that gave rise to anesthesia and antisepsis, to chemotherapy and cataract surgery. The scientific imagination is—or should be—a religious impulse" (Jenkins, 2006, 190). So, the vast array of human cultures, in all their diversity, is simply the

---

2   I acknowledge the word "culture" could describe different forms of animal behavior. While a study of animal behavior and intelligence lies beyond the scope of this work, such intelligence seems to revolve around animals' adaptability to their environments. It isn't some kind of animal "philosophy."

product of people figuring things out. This is what it means to be human, to be made in God's image, and it's the way God deals with us.[3]

Children demonstrate this questioning feature of our humanity from an extremely young age. Alison Gopnik cites experiments conducted with children between eight-months and four-years old and remarks, "Babies and very young children know, observe, explore, imagine and learn more than we would ever have thought possible. In some ways, they are smarter than adults" (Gopnik). The children in the experiments played more with toys when they had to find out how they worked, and she concludes, "Babies aren't trying to learn one particular skill or set of facts; instead, they are drawn to anything new, unexpected or informative" (*Ibid*). The difference with adults is that they are not yet goal-oriented; they are interested in everything.

Questioning is part of who we are from the very beginning. Middelmann relates this positive feature of childhood directly to our relationship with God: "When Jesus speaks of becoming like little children [Matt 18:3] . . . he blames adults for no longer having the unabashed courage to question, to demand answers, to doubt, and to discover what is true about God and human life. Adults are ashamed to stick out; for the child, it is a part of normal curiosity. And only the curious, who seek with all their heart and mind, will find and recognize the value of what they found" (Middelmann, 211-2). Curiosity, about God, is essential.

Unfortunately, some questions don't engage us with God. Typically, they are dismissive questions that drive us away rather than towards him. Isaiah likens such questioning to a pot interrogating the potter: "Woe to him who strives with him who made him, a pot among earthen pots! Does the clay say to him who forms it, 'What are you making?' or 'Your work has no handles'? Woe to him who says to a father, 'What are you begetting?' or to a woman, 'With what are you in labor?'" (Isa 45:9–10). Such

---

3   I am indebted to my colleague John Burkett for suggesting that humanity be termed "*homo-inquiricus*."

questions don't inquire—or help us in any way. They are far too "adult." They effectively tell the God of the universe, "Anything you can do, I can do better, I can do anything better than you!" John Piper warns against such questioning as he encourages Christian thinking, for the former is often characterized by "academic gamesmanship and unbelieving cynicism and indifferent dismissal" (Piper, 50). Instead, he recommends questions that are "eager to understand and believe and obey the truth" (*Ibid*). Put differently, curious child-like questions are the ones to uncover the truth.

Of course, sifting truth-seeking from dismissive questions demands thought—and that's hard work! Avoiding such effort, adults frequently choose a comfortable status quo or narrow, utilitarian goals over a careful investigation that might challenge that status quo or their cherished goals. Consequently, suppression of inquiry easily presents itself as the tempting way out. And monotheists, the supposed worshipers of the one God who made them, fall for this temptation all too often.[4] Let us consider the evidence.

---

4   Questioning in non-monotheistic cultures is a fascinating subject, but lies beyond the scope of this study. A useful work is Richard E. Nisbett's *The Geography of Thought: How Asians and Westerners Think Differently . . . and Why* (New York: The Free Press, 2003).

3
Questioning in Islam: Historically

I begin with Islam. Apart from a few exceptions, the data point to a stifling of questioning in this monotheistic tradition, from the beginning. We don't know exactly what happened,5 but according to an important hadith or tradition of Muhammad, the following interchange took place when the angel Gabriel first came to him in the cave of Hira near Mecca:

> The Prophet added, "The angel caught me (forcefully) and pressed me so hard that I could not bear it any more. He then released me and again asked me to read [or recite] and I replied, 'I do not know how to read.' Thereupon he caught me again and pressed me a second time till I could not bear it any more. He then released me and again asked me to read but again I replied, 'I do not know how to read (or what shall I read)?' Thereupon he caught me for the third time and pressed me, and then released me and said, 'Read in the name of your Lord, who has created (all that exists) has created man from a clot. Read'" (Bukhari).

This is the first revelation of what would be known as the Qur'an (or recitation). Its significance is not so much in *what* Muhammad recited as in his *having* to recite (or read). It relates to one of the most important differences between Islam and the God of the Bible. In Islam, Muhammad has to submit without question to the revelation he is given. Interestingly, as the Islamic Center of Raleigh asserts, "The word 'Islam' literally implies 'obtaining peace

---

5 I am not in a position to suggest alternatives to the Islamic traditions about Muhammad and the revelation he claimed to receive from AD 610. My purpose is simply to state and comment on the traditions, without implying that I hold them to be true.

through submission to God.' A Muslim is someone . . . who submits to God and his will."[6]

The Qur'an supports this position. Sura 49:15 commends those, "Who have believed in Allah And His Messenger, and have Never since doubted . . . Such are the sincere ones."[7] In fact, Muslims are told to forego wider questioning as they submit to quranic revelation. Sura 5:101–02 states, "O ye who believe! Ask not questions About things which, If made plain to you, May cause you trouble. But if ye ask about things When the Qur-ān is being Revealed, they will be Made plain to you, Allah will forgive those: For Allah is Oft-forgiving, Most Forbearing." The passage continues, "Some people before you Did ask such questions, And on that account Lost their faith." To put it mildly, mental engagement is discouraged. Even revelation-oriented query appears undesirable, since it has to be forgiven![8] Consequently, one's relation to the Qur'an should be characterized by submission rather than query.

On a slightly different tack, this question-stifling approach is bolstered by the Qur'an's account of Adam and the animals in Sura 2:31. Instead of Adam coming up with the names as he does in Genesis, God taught them to him.[9] So, from its earliest days, it seems Islam has discouraged questioning.

Despite these beginnings, Islam has known at least one important exception. During the eighth and ninth centuries, scholars known as Mu'tazilites ("those who withdraw") sought to satisfy the demands of both religion and reason. In other words,

---

6   This statement appeared on a flier distributed by the Islamic Center of Raleigh, North Carolina to guests attending their open house on July 25, 2009.

7   All quranic quotations are from Abdullah Yusuf Ali's translation.

8   The Arabic for "forgiven" could also be translated "obliterated."

9   "And He taught Adam the names Of all things; then He placed them Before the angels, and said: 'Tell Me The names of these if ye are right.' They said: 'Glory to Thee: of knowledge We have none, save what Thou Hast taught us: in truth it is Thou Who art perfect in knowledge and wisdom'" (Sura 2:31–32).

they believed people are endowed with the capacity to make free decisions (and by implication, to question). Robert R. Reilly explains, "The Mu'tazilites believed that God acts with purpose and his purposes are intelligible and benign. There certainly exist divine mysteries beyond man's comprehension, but God would not go against reason in His revelation in such a way as to require man to deny his reason" (Reilly, 26). Rationality is thus tentatively affirmed.

Unfortunately, the Mu'tazilites were eclipsed by others known as Mutakallimun ("those who speak in a formal manner") or Ash'arites, after Al-Ash'ari (Abu-al-Hasan Ali Ibn Ismail al-Ashari, 873–935). Stanley L. Jaki insightfully observes, Al-Ash'ari's understanding of reality cemented the essentials of the Muslim world view. In this view, reality is made up of discrete points in space and time, held together by the will of Allah, rather than by some natural law (204).[10] Any relationship in time and space, or sequence of such relationships, should be understood in terms of God's will, rather than of cause and effect. Consequently, God "could freely change the course of events according to His sole pleasure" (*Ibid*). As Reilly remarks, this means "creation exists simply as a succession of [God-induced] miraculous moments, [so] it cannot be apprehended by reason" (Reilly, 52). Consequently, all that happens is the miraculous product of an inscrutable God.

By the late eleventh century, this understanding was confirmed by the extremely influential Ash'arite, Al-Ghazali (Abu Hamid Muhammad Ibn Muhammad al-Tusi al-Ghazali, 1058–1111).[11] Reason was definitively excluded as a way of relating to God. In fact, humanity could know only God's revealed will. However, al-Ghazali was also a Sufi mystic,[12] who added an essentially subjective

10 The view may be described as "atomistic occasionalism."
11 His most influential work is *The Incoherence of the Philosophers (Tahafut al-Falasifah)*: Al-Ghazali, *The Incoherence of the Philosophers: A parallel English-Arabic text*, translated, introduced, and annotated by Michael E. Marmura (Provo, UT: Brigham Young University Press, 1997).
12 Sufis strive for a mystical oneness with God. However, for al-Ghazali, as Marmura notes, one loses oneself (i.e. experiences "annihilation") in divine

leap of faith to the supremacy of God's will. Reilly astutely points out the implications of this:

> Some form of mysticism exists in all religions. But al-Ghazali's mysticism has to be seen within the context of his having first undermined the authority of reason to know reality at all. Reason is not left as a safeguard against the potential delusions in mysticism; only the dogma of revelation is. One is then left with no means to address the more basic inquiry that the Mu'tazilites tried to undertake: Is the revelation itself reasonable? Al-Ghazali destroyed the standard by which to judge an answer to this vital question, or even to ask it in the first place (Reilly, 114).

As Jaki sums it up, al-Ghazali advocated "total surrender to the God of the Koran [sic] and to the absolute supremacy of his will in any matter however paradoxical it might appear to human reasoning" (Jaki, 205). Thus, questioning is excluded, and submission to God's revealed will, inscrutable though it may be, has directed the mainstream (Sunni) position to the present day.[13]

---

attributes which in some way are separate from God's essence: "The divine essence, at least in this world, remains for al-Ghazali beyond any human experience. . . . He further suggests that the mystical experience of 'annihilation' consists of seeing nothing in existence except the unity of all things and hence losing experience of oneself" (*Ibid*, xix).

13   It should be noted this does not apply in the same way to Shi'ites, who make up ten to fifteen percent of Muslims worldwide. Since the end of the tenth century, Shi'ites, influenced by the Mu'tazilites, have claimed revealed truth could be demonstrated by reason. See Albert Hourani, *A History of the Arab Peoples* (New York: MJF Books, 1991), 182. Unfortunately, a detailed analysis of Shi'ite approaches to reason through the ages lies beyond the scope of this work.

4
Questioning in Islam: Today

In my estimation, Islam *as such* retains its question-stifling identity. This does not exclude individual Muslims from attempts to go in a different direction. However, they are opposed by the overwhelming weight of what it has meant for centuries to be a Muslim—to submit. Typically then, while a handful of Muslim scholars question elements of Islamic practice at times, they avoid questioning Islam itself. Unfortunately, it is simply too dangerous to try. I begin with an illustration from the 1980s before moving to more recent examples.

Abdullahi An-Na'im provides a useful investigation of the views (and fate) of Sudanese scholar Mahmoud Muhammad Taha (An-Na'im, 197-224). The latter propounded the theory that Islam was originally offered on the basis of freedom of choice, and equality for all would have followed if appropriate *quranic* texts had been made the basis of the *Shari'a* (Islamic law).[14] Unfortunately, the Arabs could not live by such principles, so "the offer of freedom and responsibility was withdrawn" and texts on jihad and discrimination followed (An-Na'im, 204). Such principles became the basis of the *Shari'a*, while verses on freedom were regarded as having moral but no legal authority. As a result, this was taken "by all Muslim jurists and scholars to be the final state of affairs" (*Ibid*). Taha went on to argue the *Shari'a* today could be developed and based on the original principles of freedom and equality (*Ibid*, 205). Taha "sought to revive Islam and interpret it in a more egalitarian and tolerant way than he felt prevailed under traditional Islamic *Shari'a* law" (*Ibid*, 206). It was a noble attempt.

Considering the account of Muhammad in the cave of Hira, I suspect less freedom prevailed in incipient Islam than Taha

---

14   Texts alleged to offer freedom include Suras 16:125, 18:29 and 49:14-17.

suggested. Nevertheless, his views departed from the centuries-old pattern of submission (reinforced by Al-Ashari and Al-Ghazali), and he paid dearly. In January 1985, Taha and four disciples were sentenced to death in Khartoum. He was executed, but the others had three days to recant and were spared. The judge "ruled that the accused's views and beliefs would cause upheaval if allowed to be publicly propagated. This is the rationale for punishing religious and ideological dissent in traditional Islamic *Shari'a*" (*Ibid*, 208). Taha's case, then, highlights the difficulties one might face in seeking to move *Shari'a* in the direction of greater freedom. It certainly discourages questioning.

Moving to the twenty-first century, the views of a minority of Muslim thinkers deserve attention. An Indian Muslim, Mirza Yawar Baig, asks why Muslim institutions are so far behind in scientific and technological development, and answers, "We are a people who are the least self critical of all mankind" (Baig). Islam is not known for its self-criticism, which is why Baig's admission of that fact is notable. His admission doesn't lead him to ask whether Islam itself could be to blame though. In similar vein, the Dutch website *Nieuwemoskee* ("new mosque") aims to develop critical self-reflection within Muslim communities, arguing this characterized Islamic thinking in the past.[15] Of course this aim clashes with the stultifying effects of the Mu'tazilites' centuries-old eclipse, and the site's writers offer no hint that submission to God's inscrutable will could be the problem.[16]

On October 30, 2007, Syrian author Nidhal Na'isa came closer to questioning Islam itself, but this was not well received by Egyptian Sheikh Ibrahim Al-Khoulib. In an *Al-Jazeera*-sponsored debate between them, the interchange degenerated into an

---

15 "Nieuwemoskee streeft naar een voortgaande ontwikkeling van kritische (zelf)reflectie binnen de moslimgemeenschappen, iets wat kenmerkend was voor de vroege periode van het islamitisch denken." http://www.nieuwemoskee.nl/over/ (accessed April 20, 2011).

16 This is notwithstanding the fact that they include a number of non-Muslims.

exchange of personal insults. Na'isa sought to distinguish Islamism (which he strongly opposed) from Islam, saying, "We respect Islam in the religious, spiritual, and ideological sense" ("Al-Jazeera TV Debate on Secularism, Islamism in Arab World Deteriorates Into Exchange of Insults"). However, he found it difficult to avoid criticism of Islam when he spoke of Bedouins who invaded and destroyed great centers of civilization in Egypt, Iraq, and Syria. As Al-Khoulib rightly pointed out, those doing the invading and destroying "were the first Muslims, the companions of the Prophet Muhammad. Those are the Bedouins you are referring to" (*Ibid*). How dare Na'isa critique them! Al-Khoulib then extolled the heritage of Islam in contrast to the West, but neither man listened to the other from that point in the debate.

A slightly less provocative but nevertheless striking position is taken by Saudi intellectual Ibrahim Al-Buleihi. Like Baig, he argues that Muslims do not read their history critically. He faults the early (Islamic) Arab attitude of seeking to conquer rather than to learn, and speaks of the Arabs' "horrible delusion, this belief in one's own perfection, the belief that others must learn from them, [which] makes it impossible for them to benefit from modern culture" ("Former Saudi Shura Council member Ibrahim Al-Buleihi: The Arabs' Delusion of Their Own Perfection Makes It Impossible for Them to Benefit from Modern Culture"). However, unlike Na'isa, he avoids criticizing Islam. Speaking on an earlier occasion, he states: "We sharply distinguish between Islam in itself and what people do in its name. . . . Ever since the end of the period of the rightly-guided Caliphs, man's individuality was eradicated in Arab history" ("Saudi Intellectual: Western Civilization Has Liberated Mankind"). He has a point on the eradication of individuality, but did this begin only after the "rightly-guided Caliphs" passed from the scene? The rightly-guided Caliphs, of course, are the same individuals as Na'isa's civilization-destroying Bedouin. However, in Al-Buleihi's case, he is careful to shield those companions of Muhammad and, by extension, Muhammad himself from any criticism. This, I would assert, is inevitable in a context founded on submission.

Unfortunately, the kind of questioning exhibited by Baig, *Nieuwemoskee*, Na'isa and Al-Buleihi, even with its (mostly successful) concern not to question Islam itself, is exceptional. More typical is the stated reason behind the confiscation of Arabic books at the Riyadh International Book Fair in March 2008 by the Saudi authorities. The books concerned were blamed for spreading the *Islamic* teachings of Shi'ism and Sufism in addition to Judaism, Christianity and Buddhism. They were seen as "more dangerous to the people than lethal poison, and [so] . . . forbidden more strongly than drug smuggling, because those (drugs) corrupt the body, while these (books) corrupt religion" ("*Aafaq* Editor-in-Chief Omran Salman: Saudi Arabia Has Squandered Opportunity to Renew its Aging Political System"). This is hardly the way of free inquiry!

Finally, the situation in influential Egypt deserves mention. Although the outward circumstances surrounding the overthrow of President Hosni Mubarak on February 11, 2011 riveted Westerners' attention, the underlying reality there is particularly well captured by Geneive Abdo. During the 1990s, she spent a number of years in that country, conducting in-depth interviews (in Arabic) with people from all walks of life. She concludes that Egypt is "a society that is creating an Islamic order from the bottom up, with genuine support from the general population" (Abdo, 2000, 159). Of particular significance, though, is what she implies about Islam. She was always shown respect by the male Islamists she interviewed. However, they were not conducive to self-analysis, despite her urging, and she acknowledges that an introspective "approach is alien in Middle Eastern cultures" (*Ibid*, 17). She does not say why this is so, but provides a key hint in her discussion of Egyptian writer Sayyed al-Qimany.

Al-Qimany attempted a home-grown approach to Islam reminiscent of the ill-fated Sudanese Taha. He sought to rework Islamic tradition in his book *God of Time*. More fortunate than Taha, he only saw his book confiscated and banned. However, it would appear the contents went too close to a questioning of Islam itself. As Abdo points out, he wished to reexamine "the history of the Prophet Mohammed, the caliphs, and the origin of the *sharia*. This . . . gets to the heart of one of the major challenges. . . . To question the basis of belief is to engage in a process of examination in which the outcome is unpredictable. Although many Islamic scholars . . . are open to a reinterpretation of religious doctrine, particularly on social matters, most oppose questioning the essence of their religion" (*Ibid*, 69). This is the reality of questioning in Islam today. And the evidence indicates that in-depth engagement in Islam (i.e., responding to the questioning God, rather than submitting to the Inscrutable) will continue to be lacking.

5

Approaching Non-Questioning Islam

Islam must be recognized as the non-questioning entity it is. I acknowledge saying this is politically incorrect. However, ignoring the lack of self-critical analysis in Islam, past and present, only enhances confusion on the best way to proceed. So, two broad approaches seem helpful.

First, to the extent that Islam remains true to its essential identity it will never encourage in-depth questioning. In particular, it will remain intolerant of questions about the incomparable uniqueness of Allah and the role of his final messenger, Muhammad. One cannot submit unquestioningly and ask questions at the same time! I thus see little prospect of meaningful engagement with Islam *as Islam* on the essentials of the faith. Second, in contrast, one must not metaphorically straitjacket individual Muslims, despite their submission-oriented background. The way of the God of the Bible is to engage us as questioning beings. So Muslims should be engaged with questions, just like everyone else.

I advocate this two-fold approach against the backdrop of a vast (mostly political) literature on Islam in the West. While much of value emerges from this literature, Abdo's cautionary remarks on Islam in the West are telling. In 2007, almost a decade after her Egyptian study, she observes, "In Europe and the United States, where Muslims have maximum exposure to Western culture, they are increasingly embracing Islamic values" (Abdo, 2007). This leads her to conclude "that the future of the Islamic world will be much more Islamic than Western" (*Ibid*). In other words, Islam will continue to manifest its true self—and shield itself from scrutiny—wherever it is found.

A key example emerges from the United Nations. In March 2009, Pakistan, Saudi Arabia and other Islamic countries managed to spearhead a resolution combating defamation of religions at the United Nations Human Rights Council (UNHRC). While the resolution's title could indicate an evenhanded approach, the only religion cited for protection was Islam. Such "protection" would certainly preclude any discussion of Islam itself. Evidence for this intended result emerges from an earlier discussion in the UNHRC before the resolution was passed. The Council was examining the relationship of *Shari'a* to human rights when the Egyptian delegate forced a halt to the proceedings, insisting, "*Shari'a* law will not be [the] subject of discussion, and Islam will not be crucified in this council" ("Egyptian Liberal Magdi Khalil: Muslim Representatives Are Subverting the International Human Rights System from Within"). Apparently, analyzing Islamic law elicits strong emotions!

Interestingly, the UNHRC passed a new resolution in March 2011 to protect individuals rather than religions. It seems this change in tack was spurred by the assassination of two prominent Pakistani politicians, Salman Taseer and Shahbaz Bhatti, who had done no more than challenge that country's draconian blasphemy-of-Islam laws (Strode). Perhaps Islamic countries like Pakistan decided that the argument that Islam needed protection from individuals was untenable while the blood of the slain politicians called out from the ground. However, with greater distance from these events, I suspect Muslim countries will promote measures to protect Islam in the UNHRC once again.[17]

Muslims' refusal to subject *Shari'a* (and hence Islam itself) to any scrutiny also emerged during the visit of former President

---

17 Recent developments in the UNHRC hardly point away from the established Muslim aversion to criticism of Islam. Although a majority of respondents polled in twenty countries between April and July 2009 opposed a ban on defaming religion, most people in countries with significant Muslim populations, including Egypt, Pakistan and Iraq, agreed "criticism of religion should be prohibited." This reflects a deeply-ingrained pattern. "Majorities Reject Banning Defamation of Religion: 20 Nation Poll," *World Public Opinion*, November 20, 2009, http://www.worldpublicopinion.org/pipa/articles/btjusticehuman_rightsra/647.php?nid=&id=&pnt=647 (accessed April 29, 2011).

Mubarak to the United States in August 2009. Two press conferences were held by Coptic and Muslim Egyptians to denounce Mubarak's human rights record (Vu). There was agreement on the need for more religious freedom in Egypt, but all semblance of unity evaporated when it came to the position of *Shari'a*. Ashraf Famelah, President of Voice of the Copts, sought to point out the discrepancy between respect for (universal) human rights and the Egyptian constitution's second amendment, which provides for *Shari'a* law. The Muslims would not allow any discussion of this subject, and the proceedings degenerated into a shouting match. In sum, the evidence indicates that Islam as such is closed to meaningful engagement.[18]

A far more promising approach lies with individual Muslims. Questioning is valid simply because they, like people everywhere, are made in God's image. I admit that references to God's image contradict established Islamic theology, but we cannot avoid this fundamental difference. To clarify, there is no correspondence between God and man in mainstream Islam. As Reilly points out, "If man can know God, there must be something in him corresponding to the divine. Within Judaism and Christianity, this is not a problem, because in Genesis it states that man was 'created in God's image' . . . But this is blasphemy in orthodox Sunni Islam" (Reilly, 109). Regardless of Islamic orthodoxy, though, the questioning God of the Bible *does* engage us. He does so that we

---

18   M. Zuhdi Jasser is an interesting anomaly in this context. Described as "a devout Muslim and the president and founder of the American Islamic Forum for Democracy (AIFD)," Jasser urges "creating a liberty narrative within the Muslim conscience." "American Muslim Organization Applauds US Effort to Bring Osama Bin Laden to Justice," *AIFD*, May 1, 2011, http://www.aifdemocracy.org/news.php?id=6754 (accessed May 2, 2011). This encouragement, given right after Bin Laden's death, fits with Jasser's view that "political Islam needs to be ideologically defeated in real debate within the House of Islam." "A Muslim Soldier," *Big Peace*, July 22, 2010, http://bigpeace.com/mzjasser/2010/07/22/a-muslim-soldier/ (accessed May 2, 2011). Unfortunately, he enjoys limited support in the broader Muslim community, which shows no sign of starting a serious debate on the nature of Islam any time soon.

may know him and become his people. And that applies to Muslims, too!

In 2003, my wife and I did research on Palestinian Muslims who had turned to Christ. Using this research, a Bangladeshi control study, and literature on Muslim conversions worldwide, I found the following factors (or means) attended Muslim conversions again and again: the person of Jesus, God's supernatural involvement, the truth of Jesus' message, the role of believers, and reading the Bible (Greenham). Thus it makes sense to expect a prominent role for these factors in future Muslim conversions. As we have seen, Muslims are averse to analyzing their religion. Instead, one should focus on Jesus, expect the questioning God to act in their lives, emphasize truth (especially with key questions, as below), involve oneself personally with Muslims, and be biblical in all one says and does. Involvement in this engaging process may then lead Muslims to some analysis of Islam as well.[19]

Essentially though, and I speak specifically to Christians here, our Great Commission mandate (see Matt 28:18–20) is to make disciples of all nations, Muslims included. This is demanding and takes time. So, we should understand that before Muslims become converted disciples who have counted the cost, they typically range from being not interested through somewhat interested to seekers (Muller, 42-43).[20] However, questions may facilitate this directional process.

First, Christians should be sensitive. We should question ourselves whether a particular environment is conducive to a spiritual discussion. An individual may be reluctant to address a

---

19 My research indicates rejection of Islam is an insignificant factor in conversions to Christ. However, when the questioning God engages Muslims, unquestioning submission to Islam has to go. And that implies a degree of analysis of Islam itself.

20 An in-depth discussion of presenting the gospel to Muslims lies beyond the scope of this work. However, I recommend Muller and Georges Houssney's *Engaging Islam* (Boulder: Treeline Publishing, 2010) as excellent starting points for Muslim evangelism.

serious question when surrounded by submission-oriented others.[21] Also, in any environment, we must remember that we are addressing questioning beings made in the image of the questioning God, not walking statistics to be manipulated into buying some product.

Second, when the opportunity presents itself, the following questions may be useful: "Muslims believe in Jesus don't they?"[22] This can be a springboard to a discussion, but it could also lead to an unthinking recitation of dogma. Where there is interest, the discussion could lead to a more specific question, "What do *you* think about Jesus?" This is to determine personal interest beyond what "Muslims" believe. This could be followed by, "May I share a personal story with you?" This would be your experience of coming to know Christ. In time—and this will probably entail many lengthy discussions—one could ask the following questions: "May I tell you a story from the Bible?" This could be any gospel-oriented biblical story. Also, "Would you like to study the Bible?" One could mention Sura 10:94's admonition to Muslims to consult those who read the Book before (i.e., Christians), but this should only be used as a verbal invitation to study the *Bible*, not the Qur'an.[23] Finally, one can always ask, "Would you like to continue this conversation?"

Hopefully, such questions will lead to many ongoing conversations with Muslims, which would have a life of their own. In the meantime, we continue our investigation of monotheists by turning to Judaism.

---

21 It may also be dangerous. Although intermittently enforced, a death penalty has applied to Muslims abandoning their faith since the dawn of Islam.

22 In an initial conversation, Muslims may be more comfortable referring to him as *Nabi Isa*. By the same token, Muslims often refer to the Bible as the *Injil*.

23 Quranic studies certainly have academic merit, but I do not recommend studying the Qur'an as a way to learn about Jesus. While the quranic Jesus is highly regarded, the biblical Jesus' most important characteristics are absent there (i.e. his identity as the Son of God who died on the cross for our sins and rose again from the dead).

6
Questioning in Judaism

Unlike tendencies displayed by typical adherents of Islam, Jews as a people question intensely. This is readily seen in Jewish individuals and communities. It is a key feature of twenty-first century Judaism's astounding variety. Thomas L. Friedman remarks that the Jewish state "has a population drawn from 100 different countries, speaking 100 different languages, with a business culture that strongly encourages individual imagination and adaptation and where being a nonconformist is the norm" (Friedman). One might add to this Jews' significant diversity on religious matters, ranging from ultra-Orthodox to atheist. Unsurprisingly, an intense discussion ensues on all kinds of topics, Jewish and non-Jewish, in this vibrant arena. Friedman himself is Jewish as are most of my sources on Judaism. Their voices simply underline Judaism's characteristic questioning and self-analysis. Thinking outside the box, but also interrogating the "inside" of the box, is nothing new for the Jewish people. It all goes back to the incidence of questioning in the Jewish Scriptures but has continued strongly in Jewish tradition and culture to the present day.

A thorough historical review of Jewish questioning would need to encompass at least four thousand years. That lies far beyond our current scope. However, Yehudah Mirsky captures something of his culture's history and current identity in a review of two essays (written in Hebrew by Orthodox writers) which appeared in *Makor Rishon* on April 15th, 2011. The first essay, by Ariel Picard, contrasts two medieval scholars, the traditionalist Yehuda Halevi and the rationalist Maimonides. He argues, "The respective outlooks of these two thinkers—roughly, tradition and obedience vs. interpretation and intellectual cultivation—have vied with one another throughout the course of Jewish religious history" (Mirsky). Interestingly, Mirsky believes this presents too stark a dichotomy even within the confines of Jewish religious law (*Ibid*). The discussion nevertheless demonstrates the prevalence of intellectual ferment (i.e. questioning) in Jewish society, both past and present.

Harry Torcszyner, writing in 1924, provides another example: "As is well-known, the Jews are fond of answering a positive statement by means of a rhetorical question, which . . . conveys the correct answer to the hearer provided . . . he is able to interpret the question in the proper manner" (Torcszyner). Coming to the right conclusion by means of careful questioning is the essential idea here. This careful questioning approach also lies behind the scientific method, and Jews have certainly excelled scientifically and academically. David Brooks points to Jews making "up 0.2 percent of the world population, but . . . 27 percent of the Nobel physics laureates and 31 percent of the medicine laureates" (Brooks, "The Tel Aviv Cluster"). He admits one explanation alone cannot account for Jewish excellence, but argues "places like Silicon Valley and Tel Aviv [now a world-renowned location for entrepreneurs] are created by a confluence of cultural forces, not money." In contrast, "The surrounding nations [of the Middle East] do not have the tradition of free intellectual exchange and technical creativity" (*Ibid*). In a word, a culture of questioning, of inquiry, is crucial to scientific and research-oriented success.[24]

---

24 A related question is why the scientific revolution, which led to what we now associate with science, occurred uniquely in Europe in the Early Modern period. Unfortunately, that fascinating study lies beyond the scope of this work. It is nevertheless interesting to note Pervez Hoodbhoy's comments on science and Islam, which support the conclusions we have reached on the non-questioning nature of the latter: "Science demands a mindset that incessantly questions and challenges assumptions, not one that relies upon received wisdom. . . . Scientific progress in Muslim countries requires greater personal and intellectual freedom. Without this there can be no thinking, ideas, innovations, discoveries, or progress. The real challenge is not better equipment or faster internet connectivity. Instead, to move ahead in science, Muslims need freedom from dogmatic beliefs and a culture that questions rather than obeys." "Islam's Arrested Development," *Guardian*, November 25, 2009, http://www.guardian.co.uk/commentisfree/belief/2009/nov/25/islam-

Free inquiry is discouraged by some Jews, though, especially when authority is at stake. The ultra-Orthodox community has long been known for its seclusion from the outside world (and from other Jews, for that matter). Recently, though, a number of ultra-Orthodox websites have emerged on the Internet, only to be boycotted and in some cases shut down by community rabbis in Israel. Amy Teibel observes, "The ultra-Orthodox portals do not contain the seamy material that traditionally has been the main target of rabbinical ire. But the sites, which publish articles on politics, economics, health and religion, do offer freewheeling discussions with irreverent and unmonitored reader responses—including direct criticism of rabbis' authority" (Teibel). It would seem ultra-Orthodox rabbis oppose any discussion not strictly under their control.

In fact, the extent to which some ultra-Orthodox Jews oppose any semblance of free inquiry is seen in an apparently (but not actually) racist incident. In June 2010, around eighty Ashkenazi (i.e., European-origin) parents defied an Israeli Supreme Court ruling requiring their daughters to attend school with Sephardi (i.e., Middle East-origin) girls. However, the parents refused not because of the classmates' complexions but because they were a means of exposure to the outside world. According to Yakov Litzman, a member of an ultra-Orthodox Ashkenazi party, "There are rules of modesty, we are against the internet. . . . I don't want my daughter to be educated with a girl who has a TV at home" ("Ultra-Orthodox Jews in Mass Protest over School Ruling").

Such ultra-Orthodox attitudes should be seen as the exception to the (questioning) rule. It is far more common to see questions taking on a life of their own with or without clear direction. Erica Brown, a scholar in residence at the Jewish Federation of Greater Washington, addresses this phenomenon. Brooks highlights her

science-muslims-religion (accessed May 25, 2011). Other helpful sources include Jaki's Science and Creation and Toby E. Huff, The Rise of Early Modern Science: Islam, China, and the West 2d. ed. (Cambridge: Cambridge University Press, 2003).

approach in a context where people lack moral absolutes and seek soothing support for relativistic positions: "Jewish thinking, she says, isn't about achieving tranquility. It's about the struggle. 'I try to make people uncomfortable.'" (Brooks, "The Arduous Community"). She does this by offering "a path out of the tyranny of the perpetually open mind by presenting authoritative traditions and teachings" (*Ibid*). It seems she plays a valued role in the broader Jewish community by focusing on ultimate values but uses the means of intense, interrogative discussion to do so.

Despite concerns for the ultimate, Jewish questioning typically *encourages* the susceptibilities, if not dictates, of an always open mind. This tendency has been present for centuries. Commenting on the most comprehensive work produced by Jews, Eric S. Christianson asserts, "The Talmud is at pains to blur any distinction between holy and profane. Even more striking is that it is not concerned with answers. It is far more concerned with questions and with the *process* of answering them" (Christianson, 285). He goes on to point out the process is a spirited human argument between the human players and is even an argument with God himself (*Ibid*, 286). While God certainly allows his image-bearers to question him (as Job does), I question whether this process, this argument, leads to the God of the Bible. As we saw earlier, some questions don't engage us with God, but dismiss him instead. I'm not saying the classic Talmud, codified in late antiquity, is filled with such questions. I am saying crucial answers are inevitably elusive when the focus is on the questions rather than the questioning God. The fact remains, God has revealed himself (and questions us) in a very particular way.

Interestingly, Jews acknowledge that God has not spoken to them for millennia. Marc H. Ellis notes that "Kaddish, the Jewish prayer over the dead . . . developed during the Rabbinic Era, when God had ceased to speak." He suggests it is "the Jewish retort to a silent God—we as Jews will speak to God even though God has ceased speaking to us" (Ellis, 213). He admits the implicit defiance in this, which seems close to the dismissive, unbelieving cynicism

Piper warns against. Thus, Ellis's rather depressing conclusion comes as no surprise: "Mourning and lament are our final say to the future. Isn't this also the sign of the greatest hope? In that hope God returns. Or doesn't. God waits for us or we wait for God. Have God and the human ever been in perfect sync? . . . What God is about, when God will speak, and what God will say are beyond our power. Perhaps beyond our imagination" (*Ibid*, 225).

For all the strengths of questioning in Jewish society, Ellis's conclusion suggests questioning for its own sake, as a kind of absolute, leaves one bereft of ultimate certainty. In contrast, child-like, truth-seeking questions, the kinds God puts to and encourages from us, are indispensable. We will consider how the Jewish people respond to such questions shortly. However, a brief excursus on a core issue for the Jewish people seems helpful here. A closer look at the country of Israel should confirm whether Jewish questioning retains its vibrancy when this entity, so closely tied to Jewish identity, is the focus of discussion.

7

Questioning the Jewish State

The State of Israel, established in 1948, did not emerge from a vacuum. It embodied the dreams of Jews through the ages who wished to return to their ancient homeland. Specifically, it is the product of Zionism, a movement spearheaded by Theodor Herzl in the late nineteenth century to establish a secure home for the Jewish people in Palestine. Herzl's Zionism was influenced in large part by centuries of anti-Semitism, although this shameful phenomenon would be amplified even more in the next century's European Holocaust. Zionists saw a Jewish state in Palestine as the solution to persistent Jewish insecurity. Unfortunately, its establishment came at the expense of serious conflict with the Arab inhabitants of the region, and Palestinians typically identify the events of 1948 as the Catastrophe. The conflict continues to the present day.

Accordingly, a number of intense, opposing issues accompany any serious discussion of Israel.[25] Jews display a keen ability to identify and discuss key complexities related to the Jewish State, often with considerable disagreement. Brooks exclaims, "Israel is a country held together by argument. Public culture is one long cacophony of criticism. The politicians go at each other with a fury we can't even fathom in the U.S. At news conferences, Israeli journalists ridicule and abuse their national leaders. Subordinates in companies feel free to correct their superiors" (David Brooks, "A Loud and Promised Land"). Brooks finds this "exhausting,

---

25   A voluminous literature exists on the subject, and it is impossible to begin unraveling the issues here. While no single source can encompass everything, a useful place to begin is Colin Chapman's *Whose Promised Land? The Continuing Crisis over Israel and Palestine* (Grand Rapids: Baker, 2002). Chapman helpfully uses much original source material, reflecting a wide variety of viewpoints.

admirable, annoying, impressive and foreign," noting Israelis "blame themselves for everything" (*Ibid*). Intense questioning is alive and well, engendering great responsibility.

Such responsibility, in the midst of Israelis' ongoing conflict with the Palestinians, includes questioning themselves and what they stand for. David Ehrens reflects this well in his criticism of evangelical Mike Huckabee for supporting Israel more than American Jews do. He perceptively points out, "The fact that there are still principled Jews who fight human rights abuses—even by other Jews—is a testament to Judaism's enduring ethics, which not even the last 120 years of Zionism has managed to eclipse and corrode" (Ehrens). While many Jews would disagree with Ehrens on Zionism, there is now an interesting trend afoot to question the Zionist narrative. Traditionally this account cast Israel as the victim and blamed the Palestinians. However, reflecting on a study conducted in 2008, Rafi Nets-Zehngut points to greater Jewish willingness to share responsibility for the conflict. He suggests, "Israeli-Jewish society has changed to become more critical, open and self-reflective, allowing it to adopt less biased narratives" ("Study: Israeli Jews also blame Israel for conflict"). I believe this simply reasserts traditional Jewish values, devoted to inquiry, but the key point here is Jews' willingness to criticize their own when they are in the wrong. It is one of the greatest strengths of a culture devoted to questioning.[26]

This phenomenon of self-criticism doesn't apply to all Israelis (or Jews), of course. Just as it is wrong to suggest individual Muslims are incapable of free inquiry, so it is false to say that all Jewish individuals display this characteristic. The ultra-Orthodox cases cited above are examples. In addition, elements of Israel's settler movement are anything but self-critical. One need think no further than the adulation given to Baruch Goldstein, an Israeli settler who massacred twenty-nine unarmed Palestinians at prayer

---

26 Jesus underlines the importance of self-criticism with his instruction to remove the log from one's own eye before taking a speck from a brother's eye in Matt 7:3–5. I discuss some of its applications below.

in Hebron in February 1994. Although condemned by the Israeli government and most Israelis, his grave became a pilgrimage site, and a minority continues to praise him and his actions ("Disgusting Support for Baruch Goldstein"). It seems a narrow nationalism of the "my people right or wrong" variety lies behind such extremism. In contrast, Jews who fear such philosophical restrictiveness show a determination to stay on the path of self-criticism.

An example is (the admittedly complex) Hannah Arendt, who opposed the creation of Israel in 1948. In addition to her (realized) fears that endless violence would ensue, she was concerned that demands to support the new state would overshadow Jewish diversity. Ellis reflects the weight on her mind: "Finding comfort in the accusation that anyone who opposes the Jewish state is an anti-Semite, the state would devolve into a 'Jewish authenticity' witch hunt. This witch hunt would in turn stifle Jewish thought to the point where dissenting thought might no longer be available to the community, and unanimity of opinion would be demanded" (Ellis, 89). Ellis adds his own opposition to "theologies that currently serve to close off critical thought and favor the powerful at the expense of others" (*Ibid*, 164). One might disagree with Ellis's theological views, but these concerns certainly reflect an enduring Jewish tendency to question and criticize their own people and country.

As we leave this brief discussion of Jewish self-criticism and the State of Israel, we should note self-critical diversity isn't foolproof. Even questioning Jews have blind spots, as do we all. Examining such blind spots could produce an interesting set of perspectives on the State of Israel, but this lies beyond our current scope. Instead, there is a very common blind spot, which hinders Jews' engagement with the questioning God. To this we now turn.

8
Judaism's Most Avoided Question

By and large, despite Jews' laudable characteristic of questioning (and self-criticism), they do not welcome suggestions that Jesus is the Jewish Messiah or that they should ponder his claims. There are a number of reasons for this avoidance, which I discuss below. However, some recent examples are noteworthy.

In February 2008, several Jewish groups opposed the Roman Catholic Church for keeping (though amending) a prayer in a Good Friday liturgy, that God would enlighten Jews' hearts that they might acknowledge Jesus as Savior (Banerjee). Although the prayer is in Latin, which only a tiny fraction of Catholics understand, this did not dent Jewish criticism of the prayer's retention. The long, tragic history of Jewish persecution in Christianity's name (often under the auspices of the Catholic Church) lies behind Jews' negative reaction to the Latin prayer. At times Jews were forcibly converted to Christianity, yet were still shunned by mainstream society in a nominally Christian Europe.[27] Any hint at a resuscitation of this history, albeit unintentional, is not well received.[28]

The opposition is even greater when the question of Jesus is posed by fellow Jews in the vernacular. An Israeli polling firm, *21st Century Marketing*, asked thousands of Israelis, in Hebrew, what they thought about Jesus in early 2008. Two-thirds refused to participate once they realized what the poll was about. The 981 who did participate probably had more tolerant attitudes on the

---

27 This was certainly the case in medieval Spain. See Abraham A. Neuman, *The Jews in Spain: Their Social, Political and Cultural Life During the Middle Ages*, Vol. II, (Philadelphia: The Jewish Publication Society of America, 1948), 189–94.

28 Ongoing incidents of anti-Semitism add to Jewish fears that history might be repeated.

subject than do most Israelis. Yet even they had little interest in distinguishing Jesus' Hebrew name *Yeshua* from the more commonly known *Yeshu*, which is an acronym for the rabbinical curse, "May his name and memory be blotted out" (Brickner, "New Opinion Poll on What Israelis Think About Jesus"). Moreover, the overwhelming majority had no inkling of (or even desire to know) the central message of Jesus. In fact, only five percent had heard the claim that Jesus rose from the dead (*Ibid*)! We must highlight not only their considerable lack of knowledge here, but also their not wanting to know. It is a striking anomaly in this deeply inquisitive society.

David Brickner suggests the threat of social ostracism lies behind this anomaly, at least as far as rabbis are concerned: "Rabbis are expected to believe and teach a religion that does not accept a New Testament belief in Jesus. To inquire earnestly about whether Jesus might be the Messiah is to question the authority of traditional Jewish thought. It requires a willingness to be removed from one's chosen career and stripped of one's standing in the community" (Brickner, "A Note from David Brickner: Why Don't the Rabbis Believe in Jesus?") Of course, such consequences (and worse) have applied to all kinds of Jews entertaining Jesus' claims through the past two millennia. John Dickson explains, by the early second century, nascent Christianity was vehemently rejected by its Jewish parent: It "would no longer be considered a faction within Israel; rather, it would be seen as a perversion of Israel's faith. This was partly due to the success of yet another version of Judaism [Classical or Rabbinical Judaism, which flourished after the temple's AD 70 destruction], one that would declare the followers of Yeshua to be *minim*, or 'heretics'" (Dickson, 108).[29] Bricker adds, such opposition was apparent during Jesus' ministry, too: "After Jesus' controversial healing of the man blind from birth, John's Gospel records the Jewish leadership agreeing, 'that if anyone confessed that He was Christ, he would be put out of the synagogue' (John 9:22). Two thousand years has not changed that

---

29   It is probable that the rabbinical curse also emerged at this time.

reality one bit" (Brickner, "Why Don't the Rabbis Believe?"). Sadly, Jewish rejection of Jesus is of ancient vintage.

Nevertheless, Jesus' claims and questions should be put relentlessly to culturally inquisitive Jews. Of all people, *they* are made in the image of the questioning God![30] Engaging them is imperative. Two practical observations apply here. First, questioning Jewish society is in flux. This provides ever-changing opportunities for presenting the claims of the questioning Messiah.[31] As an example, certain contemporary Israelis called *dat'lashim* (i.e., formerly religious Jews) might entertain his questions. Mirsky describes these people as "pendant between the two worlds [of religious and secular Judaism], clearly outside the formal ambit of Orthodox authority and institutional religion generally (so that Reform and Conservative Judaism are not an option) yet still in love with its texts and intensity, and with the restlessness of their own searching" (Mirsky, "Beyond 'Religious' and 'Secular'"). Freedom from the dictates of traditional Jewish authority might facilitate their engagement with the questioning Messiah as they encounter him in the biblical text. Second, any Jew engaging Jesus should expect Jewish opposition. Despite the fact that trusting the Jewish Messiah is the most Jewish thing a Jew can do, most Jews don't see it this way at all. Some form of ostracism seems inevitable.

In the different context of Jews challenging the modern State of Israel, Ellis warns "Jews of Conscience" like himself "will be exiled from mainstream Judaism" (Ellis, 192). Unfortunately, as we have seen, his conscience leads him to questions but no certainty. It seems a great pity that Ellis and others like him should suffer

---

30   In addition, as Paul writes, to the Israelites "belong the adoption, the glory, the covenants, the giving of the law, the worship, and the promises. To them belong the patriarchs, and from their race, according to the flesh, is the Christ who is God over all, blessed forever. Amen" (Rom 9:4–5).

31   An in-depth discussion of presenting the gospel to Jews lies beyond the scope of this work. However, Michael L. Brown's multi-volume *Answering Jewish Objections to Jesus* (Grand Rapids: Baker, 2000) is useful.

exile for espousing uncertainty, principled though it may be. It would be far better to be forced out after coming to know the questioning God.

Perhaps we should conclude with the Jewish claim that God has stopped speaking. In a sense, this may be so. If God has spoken and the recipients are unyielding, what more might he have to say? Silence will ensue unless one answers his questions. Unlike many other questions, the answer here is not elusive. It is all about the one who has posed the questions from the very beginning. So I respectfully repeat the question that Jesus put to the Jews of his day: He asked, "If I tell the truth, why do you not believe me?" (John 8:46b). While the questioning God awaits an answer, we turn our attention to the third and last group of monotheists, the Christians.

9

Questioning in Catholic Christianity

Questioning by Christians is a mixed bag for the simple reason that Christians themselves vary considerably. After Jesus' death, resurrection, and ascension, his followers spread widely the good news of his saving work. Now, two millennia later, Christians of all kinds are found across the globe. Space constraints prevent serious discussion of Christian history or current Christian complexity. However, a very broad delineation places Christians in the categories of Orthodox, Catholic, and Protestant. At the risk of offending those I leave out, we pause here to consider questioning in contemporary Catholic circles before moving to (Evangelical) Protestantism.[32]

A hugely significant process of questioning and reformulation in the Catholic Church took place at (and following) the Second Vatican Council of 1962–65. While it affirmed traditional church doctrines, the Council provided remarkably new perspectives on how they might be viewed. Catholic writer Paul E. Dinter observes, Vatican II "explicitly accepted historical change as the normative context for understanding and appropriating the ancient faith of the church" (Dinter, 1). It marked a break with Catholicism's "past,

---

32 A fascinating study, beyond the scope of this work, would concern the role questioning, or free inquiry, has played in holding Christians together and driving them apart, through the ages. Key events to consider include (but are not limited to) Christianity becoming the religion of the Roman Empire in the fourth century, the Trinitarian and Christological controversies of the fourth and fifth centuries, the break between Western and Eastern churches in the eleventh century, and the sixteenth century Reformation. Questioning aside, alignment with such events also marks Christians as orthodox or otherwise, whether such orthodoxy is seen theologically or organizationally (as in the Orthodox Church). This chapter's focus simply reflects the huge influence Catholicism has had and continues to have worldwide, without denigrating the impact of other traditions.

accepting some of the Reformation's program, employing historical-critical perspectives, and admitting the reality of progress, development, and pluralism . . . as it proceeded to make new applications of the tradition" (*Ibid*, 2). Space does not allow even a basic treatment of Vatican II's impact on Catholicism. However, it created tension between some traditionalists clinging to long-standing church dogma and many others embracing new opportunities for discussion. Our look at questioning in Catholicism thus occurs in this broad context.[33]

Choosing a few specific topics in any wide context is risky. However, Richard P. McBrien identifies three areas which mark off Catholics from other Christians: sacramental, mediation, and communal (McBrien, 9). Each of these presents opportunities for questioning. We will consider transubstantiation as it emerges from the sacramental, the mediation of Mary, and conversion in a communal setting.

The Catholic Church plays a key sacramental role itself. McBrien emphasizes that the Church is "the fundamental sacrament of our encounter with Christ," but sees individual sacraments *of* the Church as the visible means by which "encounter with Christ is expressed, celebrated, and made effective" (*Ibid*, 10).[34] This encounter is particularly prominent in the Eucharist, a ritual meal of bread and wine. Protestants generally see this ritual as a simple commemoration of Christ's death on their behalf (and often substitute grape juice for wine), but Catholics see it as the embodiment of Jesus' presence in the congregation. Monika K. Hellwig explains that medieval Catholics were at pains to assert the

---

33 The expansive context for questioning in 21st Century Catholicism also includes the presence of many Catholic universities (in the United States and beyond) with a long-standing reputation for excellence in higher education. Unfortunately, it also includes a clergy sex-abuse scandal, which has attracted intense questioning from Catholics and non-Catholics alike. Discussing these positive and negative aspects lies beyond our current scope.

34 Traditionally, sacraments such as baptism, confirmation, the Eucharist, penance, anointing the sick, matrimony, and holy orders were seen as visible signs of an invisible grace.

real presence of Christ in the Eucharist and so insisted that Jesus'
figurative words "this is my body" (in Matt 26:26, Mark 14:22, and
Luke 22:19) be understood literally when spoken by the officiating
priest. Thus, transubstantiation is supposed to occur with the bread
becoming the body of Christ (Hellwig, 144).[35] Since Vatican II,
though, the focus has been on what should happen to the
community of faith rather than what might happen to the elements.
So, Hellwig asserts that the Eucharist "points to the presence of
Jesus in the word of Scripture that is read, in the faith of the
community that is gathered to participate and in the action and
things used, which are the outreach of Jesus himself who initiated
this celebration . . . to touch his followers in the most intimate
communion" (*Ibid*, 145-46). The emphasis is on a multi-faceted
presence of Christ.

Despite Hellwig's (post-Vatican II) emphasis, many Catholics
see Jesus' presence in the Eucharist more literally. Protestant
Canadian Prime Minister Stephen Harper discovered this after
attending a Catholic funeral (which included the Eucharist) in 2009
(Lewis). Since he was sitting in the front row, he was given the bread
(also called the host) in the form of a wafer. A dispute ensued over
whether he put it in his mouth or in his pocket. His office insisted
he swallowed it, but the issue was not how he disposed of a symbol,
but what he did to Jesus himself. As Neil MacCarthy, Director of
Communications of the Archdiocese of Toronto, asserted, "The
Communion wafer starts as a host and becomes the body of Christ.
. . . We believe we are holding Jesus in our hands so to put Jesus in
your pocket or to put Jesus on the ground [is serious]. . . . We never
throw Jesus out" (*Ibid*). MacCarthy would probably agree with
Hellwig on Christ's multi-faceted presence, but his assertion that
a wafer *is* the physical Jesus, who can be pocketed or thrown out,
seems to lack Catholicism's more recent questioning approach.

---

35 She provides more detail on how transubstantiation was understood in
its medieval and subsequent contexts on pp. 143–45.

Somewhat less questioning applies to Mary.[36] McBrien reminds us that an encounter with God must be mediated. While the human Jesus is the ultimate God-conveying Mediator, Catholics see Mary, the human mother of the divine Jesus, as an instrument of God as well. They may thus ask her to intercede for them (McBrien, 11-12). Hellwig explains this in terms of Mary being a positive example for the struggling Church. Since she was conceived immaculately (i.e., sinless, albeit through Jesus' anticipated merits) and was assumed bodily into heaven, Christians can be assured that redemption and heaven are ultimately attainable for them too (Hellwig, 124). Thus, Catholics are encouraged to venerate (i.e., pray to, but not worship) Mary because God's grace has triumphed preeminently in her. Catholics' unity with Mary expresses the (imperfect) Church's collective union with Christ (McBrien, 1104-09). She thus embodies their future hope too.

Unfortunately, the preeminence given to (sinless) Mary would imply that lesser mortals (i.e., sinners in the Church) cannot be sure of their redemption or the triumph of God's grace in them. Interestingly, Dinter critiques a literal understanding of a sinless Mary because it "weakens at its heart the evangelical tenor of the doctrine of grace. Understood symbolically, the doctrine makes Mary the first of the 'first to hope in Christ,' without her maternal singularity making her a demigod" (Dinter, 291). However, Dinter needs to be careful for Pope Pius IX (1846–78) and Pope Pius XII (1939–58) explicitly declared deniers of the Immaculate Conception and Assumption to have left the Catholic faith. These solemn papal declarations were left untouched by Vatican II (McBrien, 1102-04). Catholics are thus more inclined to elevate Mary, even to inappropriate demigod status, than risk questioning the dogmas of her preeminence. Sadly, such undue elevation of

---

36 A thorough study of Catholic teaching on the mother of Jesus, including her so-called Immaculate Conception and Assumption, lies beyond our current scope. Dinter, *Beyond Naive Belief*, 254–60, provides a useful, if somewhat liberal, discussion on the history of these doctrines.

Mary easily eclipses the present sufficiency of salvation in Christ for imperfect run-of-the-mill believers (like me).

In contrast to all this, the Bible clearly states that Christ's salvation is sufficient for individual sinners who turn to God on his terms (i.e., convert) right now. For instance, Jesus tells the newly converted tax collector Zacchaeus that salvation had come to him that day, implying he was no longer lost but found (Luke 19:8–10). Similarly, Peter's report that the gentile Cornelius and his household had received the Holy Spirit led the Jewish church in Jerusalem to conclude that they were truly saved on believing in Christ (Acts 11:14–18). Later in Philippi, the jailer's positive response to Paul and Silas's admonition to believe in the Lord Jesus to be saved led to his rejoicing that he had done so (Acts 16:31–34). In each case, the biblical text indicates that salvation was a present possession of the converted individuals.

Regrettably, Catholic writers give the impression that conversion (and hence salvation) is an interminable process.[37] Ronald D. Witherup implies a lack of finality, if not assurance, when he argues, "most conversions appear to be a *process* on some line of continuum. The message for disciples is that it [conversion] is an ongoing process, a journey of faith, that requires constant attention" (Witherup, 109). I agree that my faith requires constant attention, but I attend to it *because* of my conversion, not as part of it. Similarly, Hellwig says the Church comprises sinful individuals who are still "in the painful and laborious process of personal conversion" (Hellwig, 123). It seems that she confuses conversion with perfection (or complete sanctification), which is certainly not a believer's possession in this life. However, her argument that individuals in the Church are "only partially converted," weakens the good news that I may be transformed (i.e., saved) as I turn to Christ in humble surrender, right now (*Ibid*).

---

37 I acknowledge that conversion is a process. For instance, it took several days for both Saul of Tarsus and Cornelius to be fully converted (see Acts 9:3–20 and 10:1–48). However, it is not a never-ending process. I discuss this and the biblical nature of conversion in Greenham, *Muslim Conversions to Christ*, 11–27.

Catholicism's communal focus would explain Witherup and Hellwig's presentation of an incomplete conversion. McBrien reminds us that the Church mediates "salvation through sacraments, ministries, and other institutional elements" (McBrien, 13). Thus, those who participate in the Church's sacraments, ministries, and institutional elements might consider themselves on a path of ongoing, unfinished conversion. Any greater assurance is elusive—and its effective absence unquestioned.

In response to this uncertainty, and to conclude our discussion on Catholicism, I have a biblical question. In 2 Corinthians 13:5, Paul has the following instruction for people in the church of Corinth: "Examine yourselves, to see whether you are in the faith. Test yourselves. Or do you not realize this about yourselves, that Jesus Christ is in you?—unless indeed you fail to meet the test!" The question is not whether they belonged to the church and participated in its ministries. They did all that. The question was whether they were in the faith and Christ was in them. In other words, were they truly converted, then and there, despite their imperfections and sin? So, with all respect, my question to people in the Catholic (or any other) Church is this: Have you allowed sacraments, Church mediation, or communal activity (whatever its nature) to replace coming to know the questioning God in biblical conversion? I pray that questions such as this would lead to a true knowledge of him.

10
Questioning and Evangelicalism

Finally, we turn to Evangelical Christians. Simply put, evangelicals are those who cling to the biblical Jesus for salvation.[38] I am an evangelical. The presuppositions behind my use of the Scriptures—the Scriptures which reveal the questioning God to us—are all evangelical. However, if I truly believe in (i.e., respond to) this God, questioning is central.

God certainly questioned that highly prominent convert Saul who later became Paul. In an interview with *Christianity Today's* John Wilson, Sarah Ruden argues that Paul's conversion is foundational to questioning in Western culture:

> What characterizes our society at its best is the habit of looking at ourselves with a critical attitude. I think this really started for Western civilization on the road to Damascus. Paul is doing what he's expected to do in his environment . . . [then] he is forced to answer the questions, *What are you doing? What are you actually doing? Why are you persecuting me?* . . . So there's a galvanizing, horrifying, but enlightening realization that what you do every moment you do in the sight of an infinitely loving God. . . . And I think that has made us who we are religiously and ethically (Wilson).

Paul's Jewish background would surely have prepared him for his encounter with the questioning God. However, Ruden points

---

38   While the scope of this work does not allow a discussion of questioning among non-evangelical Protestants, evangelicals are found across a number of Protestant denominations and may include Catholics. Alister E. McGrath identifies evangelicals in terms of their biblical, redemptive, conversionist and evangelistic assumptions in *Christian Theology: An Introduction*, 4th ed. (Malden, MA: Blackwell Publishers, 2007), 80–81.

persuasively to the role of divinely-inspired questioning for Christianity and the Western civilization it influenced.

Within this broad Western context, David Bentley Hart points to "the long and honorable tradition of Christianity's critical examination and reexamination of its own historical, spiritual, and metaphysical claims" (Hart, 101). In particular, vibrant evangelical faith must ask and answer this question: Did God raise Jesus from the dead? I must be convinced that he did if I am to surrender to Jesus as the bearer of my sin and the ever-living Lord of the ages. Colin Thubron remarks, when no one doubts, the difference between those who accept or forget their faith is miniscule: "A living belief must survive questions" (Thubron, 124). However, a successful evaluation of the claims of the faith should be followed by another question. Once I have turned to him in conversion I, like the apostle Paul, must ask, "What shall I do, Lord?" (Acts 22:10a).

What the Lord would have me do is a question to repeat throughout my life as a believer. There are many ready answers in the Scriptures of course, but a lifestyle of questioning is certainly implied. As Jesus admonishes his disciples, "Ask, and it will be given to you; seek, and you will find; knock, and it will be opened to you" (Luke 11:9). We discern his gracious purposes for us as we ask, seek, and knock.[39] This should come as no surprise. We have already seen that people made in God's image are called to respond to him in the context of mental and spiritual engagement. When we are redeemed in Christ, the pattern is no different. Piper clarifies, "The Lord never says, 'Stop thinking about my Word; I'll tell you what this means'" (Piper, 51). Thinking is the way for his people.

Unfortunately, popular evangelical piety easily discourages a questioning lifestyle. Consider Jerry Bridges' admonition: "The Scriptures do not allow for *any* gossip or criticism, or any other form of unwholesome speech, even if what we say is true"

---

39 I discuss these principles at greater length in their Matt 7 context below.

(Bridges, 35). He rightly addresses the danger of nurturing a destructively critical spirit. Middelmann would concur, acknowledging the enduring importance of humility. However, Middelmann adds we mustn't falsely prioritize humility "when a life is threatened or careful plans need to be drawn up to avoid a catastrophe" (Middelmann, 107). He wisely points out, "The remedy for arrogance is not humility, but more careful insight" (*Ibid*, 106). Regrettably, in asserting biblical condemnation of unwholesome speech, Bridges overlooks specific Scriptures which, quite frankly, encourage critical evaluation. Examples include Paul's remarks to Titus on Cretans being "liars, evil beasts, lazy gluttons" (Tit 1:12), and Jesus' cutting words of condemnation addressed to the hypocritical scribes and Pharisees in Matthew 23. It is evident that a critical evaluation of those first century communities is biblical. Such evaluation emerges naturally from a questioning lifestyle.[40]

Apart from the effects of a misunderstood piety, evangelicals typically don't question authority. David P. Gushee observes, "Evangelicals have been schooled on a traditional reading of the biblical text Romans 13:1–7, which tends toward a high degree of respect for, trust in, and subordination under, government authority, especially in its exercise of the 'sword,' that is, state violence. This is related to a broader evangelical authoritarianism, especially in our most conservative quarters" (Gushee, 75-76). Such authoritarianism doesn't apply to all evangelicals, of course, but the position each of us reaches on the subject must be biblically determined.[41] As a general rule, submission to the ruling authorities is obligatory because God put them there (Rom 13:1), but this

---

40 I discuss how to attempt a lifestyle of critical evaluation below.
41 Space constraints prohibit a thorough discussion of Christians and authority, including the complexity of church-state relationships. A useful source is Timothy Samuel Shah's chapter, "For the Sake of Conscience: Some Evangelical Views of the State," in *Church, State, and Citizen: Christian Approaches to Political Engagement*, ed. Sandra F. Joireman (Oxford: Oxford University Press, 2009), 113–43.

submission occurs in a context of law and order (Rom 13:3-4).[42] So it seems our submission is designed to enhance the kind of civic stability Paul urges us to pray for in 1 Timothy 2:1–7, viz., a peaceful context where people may come to know and serve God through Jesus. Finally, as we submit, we do so as free people, ultimately accountable to God (1 Pet 2:16).[43] To summarize, a New Testament approach to power or authority would imply questions on whether it enhances stability and provides freedom for people to encounter God. It also asks whether believers display a God-dependent freedom and dignity, regardless of the justice of the authority at hand. Unthinking submission is excluded.

If biblical questioning is the right approach, suppressing inquiry of the status quo remains an easy temptation. The evidence suggests that evangelicals are susceptible to it. Mark A. Noll disturbingly remarks, "No body of Christians has been as capable at exercising power as American believers, though few have been more reluctant to address questions of power face-on" (Noll, 59). This reluctance, together with a general lack of questioning, has serious effects. We now turn to these consequences.

---

42 Without addressing all the scenarios which might arise, Rom 13:1–7 would not endorse the whims of a gang leader who temporarily has the upper hand in a context of lawlessness, although wisdom might suggest (temporary) acquiescence in some of his demands. On the other hand, duly constituted states often have unjust or immoral laws. In that case, when a Christian has no choice, he or she should obey God rather than men (as Peter did in Acts 5:29ff.), and then face the consequences.

43 Accountability to God is also the essential idea behind Jesus' response to the Jewish leaders questioning him on paying taxes to Caesar (in Matt 22:15–22). If payment of a coin with Caesar's image was due to Caesar, a much greater obligation rests on every human being made in *God's* image: We owe all we are to him.

11

Repercussions of Non-Questioning Evangelicalism

Without a questioning lifestyle, all kinds of things go unnoticed. A panel at Southern Baptist Theological Seminary alluded to this problem in a discussion of Neil Postman's *Amusing Ourselves to Death* in March 2011 (Postman). Acknowledging the generally negative effects of television on serious thinking, Mark Coppenger, one of the panelists, pointed a finger at his fellow evangelicals: "We haven't had the Jesuits or the Jewish rabbi pounding us enough and so we become, I think, kind of weak and insipid, where we can pontificate and then take notes or then just lash back and then not be discursive" (Hayes).

In fact, the lack of thinking underlying this evangelical phenomenon shows itself especially in an unwillingness to question one's own. Robert F. Kennedy famously told a South African audience in 1966, "For every ten men who are willing to face the guns of an enemy there is only one willing to brave the censure of his colleagues, the wrath of his society" (Massie, 202). Whether Kennedy's ratio holds or not, the risks of critiquing the way my group operates are easily outweighed by the appeal of unthinking submission. But the latter dehumanizes us since we are made in the image of the questioning God. It also hinders our witness to that questioning God. So I focus here on the consequences of evangelicals accepting certain Christian positions (and leaders) unquestioningly. I examine such effects in the contexts of international relations, a Christian institution, and the local church.

A significant case of hindered Christian witness emerges from the enthusiastic but poorly considered embrace of evangelical President George W. Bush's invasion of Iraq. Internationally, Christian leaders opposed Bush's invasion plans, but their voices were drowned in a tide of patriotic endorsement. Reflecting on this support (which included 87 percent of white evangelicals in April 2003), Charles Marsh asks, "Why did American evangelicals not pause for a moment in the rush to war to consider the near-unanimous disapproval of the preemptive attack by the global Christian community" (Marsh, 182)? The global Christian community (like American evangelicals) can certainly be mistaken, but refusal even to hear the views of believers elsewhere speaks of ungodly arrogance. It also held devastating implications for the longstanding presence of Christians—a witness in itself—in the Fertile Crescent. Marsh points out, "A Christian community of nearly a million lived in Iraq under Saddam Hussein's repressive regime. However, few of us in the evangelical churches asked the Christians in Iraqi churches what they thought of our plan for the Middle East" (*Ibid*, 167). As a result, one of the greatest catastrophes following the 2003 invasion was the loss of over half that country's Christian population.[44]

Without doubt, Muslim extremists were directly responsible for this loss. However, even limited inquiry into past and present Middle East realities would show the dangers of Western military interference for Christian minorities in the region. *Barnabas Aid* observes, "There is a saying among Christians in the Middle East that every time Europeans intervene in the Middle East the indigenous Christians suffer" ("Iraq: The Betrayal of the Christians", 6).[45] This enduring reality was ignored, and the peril for Middle East Christians continues.[46]

---

44 Many reliable sources convey this broad statistic, including Aamer Madhani's citation of the UNHRC in "For Christians in Iraq, the Threats Persist," *USA Today*, June 2, 2010, http://www.usatoday.com/news/world/iraq/2010-06-01-iraq-christians_N.htm (accessed June 28, 2011).

45 Philip Jenkins provides helpful historical background to this phenomenon in *The Lost History of Christianity: The Thousand-Year Golden Age of the Church in the Middle East, Africa, and Asia—and How It Died* (New York: HarperOne, 2008).

46 This is not the place to attempt an analysis of the George W. Bush (or any) presidency. However, evangelicals should not assume a president who calls him- or herself a Christian automatically acts biblically or furthers God's Kingdom. Vigilant questioning, as opposed to blind loyalty (because he's "our guy"), can alert a Christian president to the possibility of biblical alternatives, whether the administration adopts them or not.

Reporting on yet another Christian murder in Iraq in mid-2011, *Barnabas Aid* points to a new dilemma for those still hoping to flee their homeland: turmoil in Christian-minority countries like Syria, which until recently accommodated refugees ("Second Iraqi Christian Murdered in Two Weeks"). I have no easy solutions for the plight of such Christians in the second decade of the twenty-first century. It is extremely difficult to craft a policy which accommodates the legitimate interests of current rulers, Muslim majorities, and Christian and other minorities in that volatile region. However, evangelical enthusiasm for any action which ignores Christians there is wrong. It not only despises those Christians, it also dishonors the one who died for them, and for us.

Moving closer to home, it seems harder to question leadership when the leaders control one's personal welfare. In a well-publicized 2007 case, three professors at Oral Roberts University (ORU) in Tulsa, Oklahoma were dismissed after alerting the administration to a number of improprieties. In the ensuing dust-up, the president was replaced, the board of regents restructured, and the school reached confidential settlements with the professors.[47] Regardless of the accusations' veracity, the sweeping nature of ORU's changes indicates something was seriously amiss. Had appropriate internal questioning been welcome, ORU might have avoided an embarrassing public scandal. John W. Kennedy highlights the case of Tim Brooker, one of the terminated professors. Brooker alerted the administration to moral and financial issues of concern, but heard nothing for over a year: "Finally . . . he pointed out a pattern of lavish spending among the school's administrative leaders. A month later . . . he was forced out" (Kennedy). It wasn't long before ORU's problems were all over the secular media.

In the wake of the scandal, the ongoing question is whether a heavy-handed approach reemerges or one which encourages and

47 Matthew Avery Sutton provides useful background in "Oral Surgery," *Religion in the News* 10.3 (Winter 2008), http://www.trincoll.edu/depts/csrpl/RINVol10No3/Oral%20Surgery.htm (accessed June 29, 2011).

responds to legitimate concerns. Kennedy asks of ORU, "Can it overcome what former provost Mark Lewandoski publicly called a 'culture of fear,' a reference to faculty and staff anxieties about bringing up problems to the administration" (*Ibid*)? One would hope Christian institutions like ORU live up to their Savior's name. In the spirit of Romans 8:15, this means recognizing that every believer has been adopted by the questioning God, and so should be heard. It does not mean trying to control people through fear.

Finally, pandering to whatever people want is detrimental, too. Regrettably, a form of "the customer is always right" mentality has found its way into the local church. D.H. Williams laments, "State-of-the-art ministry, we are told, should be about the business of assessing the needs of potential religious consumers and meeting those needs. The church is thus viewed as 'a service agency' which exists to satisfy people's needs, and its success is measured by how well it is fulfilling this goal" (Williams, 212-13). This approach is pervasive. Gary E. Gilley adds, "The most successful arm of the evangelical church in recent years, in terms of growth, money and prestige, has been the market-driven (seeker-sensitive, new-paradigm, user-friendly) church. Because of this success these churches are being mimicked all over the country, and indeed, the world" (Gilley, 13). Few question their outward success, even if truth is displaced by an unbiblical focus on self-esteem (*Ibid*, 61). However, making people feel good about themselves is not the way they come to know the God who loves them and, therefore, radically questions them. Self-celebration is antithetical to conversion.

Reflecting this concern, Gilley asks serious questions about an un-churched lady who is supposedly coming to Christ:

> [Assuming she] does not clearly understand that the real issue on the table is her personal sinfulness that has offended a holy and righteous God, does she understand the gospel at all? If she believes that Christ died on the cross to save her from a poor self-image in order to give her a fulfilling life brimming with excitement, has she

not been presented with a gospel so hopelessly muddled that the true gospel is still a mystery to her [?] Can such a person, who so totally misunderstands the purpose and nature of Calvary, be saved, even though she has prayed the "sinner's prayer"? From my understanding of the true gospel I would have to say probably not (*Ibid*, 72-73).

The gospel presents the Christ who saves me from my sin, not a god devoted to my personal fulfillment. Kent Philpott echoes Gilley's disquiet, but focuses more closely on means. He concedes folks may be converted (i.e., saved) "after saying a prayer, coming forward, raising their hand, or being baptized" (Philpott, 47). However, these measures do not in themselves convert anyone. Biblical conversion is the transformation which occurs as an individual turns to Christ in humble surrender, encountering him by the power of God (Greenham, 27). Philpott rightly asserts, "When we come to Jesus for forgiveness and salvation because the Holy Spirit has convicted us and shown us Jesus as the remedy, we look to Jesus—and not to any other person or institution—as the source of our salvation" (Philpott, 49).

It is grossly irresponsible to claim outward means, like saying a formulaic prayer, automatically and inevitably bring salvation, whether the people concerned truly trust in Christ or not. Unthinkingly declaring God's approval, just because folks feel good or said the "right words," has serious, eternal consequences. A Jesus who unconditionally affirms me is not the questioning Christ of the Bible. The real one died and rose to *have* me—but only on his terms.

Since there are always repercussions, it is important that evangelicals ask questions (i.e., think things through), but we must do so biblically. Piper reminds us, "If we abandon thinking, we abandon the Bible, and if we abandon the Bible we abandon God" (Piper, 123). However, before questioning others, including our leaders, we must question ourselves. And this brings us to a biblical passage that helpfully sets out the way to do it.

12
A Biblical Way Forward

Jesus' words in the latter part of the Sermon on the Mount provide several principles for a biblical, questioning lifestyle. First, he admonishes his followers not to judge (Matt 7:1), adding (with hyperbole) we must remove logs from our own eyes before attempting to remove specks from our brothers'. He then cautions us not to "give dogs what is holy" or cast "pearls before pigs" (Matt 7:6) before advocating a process of constant asking, seeking, and knocking. This leads to the so-called Golden Rule, that we do to others what we would have them do to us (Matt 7:12).

Questioning is prominent in this passage. It by no means exhausts its meaning or application, but it does tie the passage together. So to begin, we never take the place of our questioning God. Judging (or condemning) is the Lord's sole prerogative, which he will exercise in an ultimate sense. As Paul tells the Corinthians, "Do not pronounce judgment before the time, before the Lord comes" (1 Cor 4:5a). All too often, our questioning is more answering (i.e., condemning) than enquiring, and the sense in the Greek is to stop the judging we've already started. However, as we stop jumping to premature—and damning—conclusions, we don't stop questioning. The questioning simply starts with us.

Self-questioning (i.e., removing "logs" from our eyes) is penetrating and devastating. It is no less demanding than questioning the basis of Islam for a Muslim, or considering Jesus as Messiah for a Jew. It leads to the discovery that I am defiled, since "out of the heart of man, come evil thoughts, sexual immorality, theft, murder, adultery, coveting, wickedness, deceit, sensuality, envy, slander, pride, foolishness. All these evil things come from within, and they defile a person" (Mark 7:21–23). This isn't pleasant, but Jesus came to take the evil of the likes of me: "For our sake [God] made him to be sin who knew no sin, so that in him we might become the righteousness of God" (2 Cor 5:21). We have to make this discovery and turn to Jesus, who died on the cross for our sins and rose again from the dead, to cleanse us. That's biblical conversion.

Thereafter, as we get to know our questioning God better, rigorous self-questioning remains the doorway to wider evaluation. Only then can we see clearly enough to remove specks from the eyes of others and to identify those whom Jesus calls dogs and pigs. What does that entail? Arrogance is always excluded, but questioning is central. As a matter of fact, the word translated "see clearly" in Matthew 7:5 implies taking in everything around you, including things in your peripheral vision.[48] Thus, careful consideration of other people's circumstances, seen in the light of my own failings, is required for me to help them. Unfortunately, some are not candidates for speck removal, but are dogs and pigs. D.A. Carson suggests the latter are people "who have given clear evidences of rejecting the gospel with vicious scorn and hardened contempt" (Carson, 185). We must discern who they are.[49] When it comes to sharing biblical truth, we cannot assume all people are the same, but should treat them differently.

We obtain more insight into all this in the next part of the passage as Jesus tells us to "Ask, and it will be given to you; seek and you will find; knock, and it will be opened to you" (Matt 7:7). The sense in the Greek is to keep on asking, seeking and knocking. It is not a one-off activity: Things are not delivered to us, ready-formed on a platter. Thinking is required! However, the principle of constant questioning applies in at least two ways. First, it

---

48   The root word διαβλέπω may be translated "look intently," "open one's eyes (wide)" or "see clearly." Walter Bauer, William F. Arndt, F. Wilbur Gingrich and Frederick W. Danker, *A Greek-English Lexicon of the New Testament and Other Early Christian Literature* 2d. ed. (Chicago: University of Chicago Press, 1979), 181.

49   The questioning implied here also emerges later in the chapter when Jesus says we would know (or recognize) false prophets by their fruits (Matt 7:15–20). That's impossible without inquiring who they might be.

determines how I deal with other people and, second, how I discover God's ongoing will for my life.

Looking back at the previous verses, I must inquire (by asking, seeking, and knocking) whether individuals I encounter may be helped and, if so, how. There are dogs and pigs out there. They should be approached with care. But despite the evil in humanity, we are all made in the image of the questioning God. So whatever the situation, I should ask questions like these: "What is the nature of evil here?" and "What positive difference can I make?" but also "Is there a question I can ask, as the questioning God seeks to engage people in this situation?" In other words, we must follow Jesus' admonition to remove specks prudently, but also withhold pearls of vulnerable truth when appropriate. Randy Newman advises, "We should choose our questions carefully, depending upon where our friends stand on the path toward the Cross. Listening to their answers can help us determine this point and move them further along" (Newman, 243). A discerning approach is essential.

Then, moving forward, I pursue the "Lord, what do you want me to do?" question. This means I follow a path of constant investigation. It is a path believers take with confidence because Jesus assures us that our "Father who is in heaven [will] give good things to those who ask him!" (Matt 7:11). Essentially, we must explore before we receive. Carson observes that God uses the means of asking, seeking, and knocking "to teach his children courtesy, persistence, and diligence" (Carson, 186) Put differently, those who have come to know the questioning God keep pursuing him (by asking, seeking and knocking). Paul also advocates this exploratory approach in a number of his epistles. One might think his acquaintance with the supernatural could exempt him (and his hearers) from the hard work of questioning and trying things out, yet he urges: "Be transformed by the renewal of your mind, that by *testing* you *may discern* what is the will of God" (Rom 12:2), also "*try to discern* what is pleasing to the Lord" (Eph 5:10), and "Do not despise prophecies, but *test* everything; hold fast what is good"

(1 Thes 5:20–21).[50] Quite simply, testing and exercising discernment are the way we pursue the questioning God's specific purpose for us.

Finally, it is God's will, "whatever you wish . . . others would do to you, do also to them" (Matt 7:12). Piper notes that this command (the Golden Rule) begins with the word "so." It does not stand alone but rests on what has gone before. Thus, we should treat others the way we would like to be treated *because* we have a loving heavenly Father who provides our needs (Piper, 53). The logic of this principle applies to the passage's questioning motif as well. Since our questioning God wants us to ask, seek, and knock as we look for his provision, we should encourage others to do the same. By now I should *want* to be engaged as a questioning being, so I should treat you as a questioning being also.[51]

In sum, this passage's engaging thrust is inescapable. The questioning God confronts us, but in doing so expects us to behave as questioning beings. We must ask questions in humility in the context of knowing him, but this is the way for everyone. Then if we care for others, and we must, we should encourage them on the path of ongoing God-directed questioning too.

---

50   In each verse, the word or words italicized translate δοκιμάζω. Meanings include "put to the test, examine" or "discover." BAGD, *Greek-English Lexicon*, 202.

51   A similar idea emerges with the command to love one's neighbor as oneself in Lev 19:18. One should "reason frankly with" (or rebuke) one's neighbor (vs. 17). Love requires engagement—not a grudging silence!

13
Living It Out

To conclude, how do you put into practice these principles for a biblical, questioning lifestyle? First, you must believe questioning is important. If you don't, if it's okay to "go with the flow," do you really know the questioning God of the Bible? If you do know him though, developing a questioning lifestyle is non-negotiable. This biblically-driven lifestyle is all-encompassing and demanding, extending well beyond what I can cover here. A quick look at critical evaluation in the home, church, and society will hopefully do for now.

First, Christian homes should be characterized by love and (an orderly) security, centered on the Lord Jesus Christ. Obedience engenders orderliness, but as parents teach it to their children, they may provoke them to anger as Paul implies in Ephesians 6:4. Since he contrasts this problem with raising them "in the discipline and instruction of the Lord," I believe it boils down to whether questions are encouraged or not. The Lord's discipline and instruction certainly entail questioning, as we have seen, but stifling truth-revealing curiosity easily leads to anger (and discouragement, cf. Col 3:21). I can think of no worse basis for discipline in a Christian home than the words, "Because I say so!" This simply teaches a child that the one with more power gets to order around those with less. That's not the way we come to know the questioning God! Without minimizing a parent's God-given authority, let me suggest a better way.

I teach a sizable adult Sunday school class, and after giving them time to socialize, I ring a little bell to call them to order and get the session started. It causes some amusement, but they expect me to ring it and won't stop talking until I do. One Sunday, Andrew, a teenager in the class (we have one or two), wanted to ring the bell early in our socializing time. I asked him why I rang the bell. He took that as a no and turned to go, but I insisted he answer my question. He said it was to get the class started. I asked if it was time to start class. He agreed it was not and so had a good reason why he shouldn't ring the bell. When it *was* time to start, I let him ring it, even though doing so is my trademark activity. That way, I didn't put the kid down but achieved orderliness with understanding. In a way, I took the "log" out of my eye by not insisting on my right to ring the bell and took the "speck" out of Andrew's by making him think through the wisdom of his request.

Applying this simple illustration to a home environment, we should ensure that we give our children good reasons for our instructions and even welcome questions about them. Eva and I brought up our kids this way. In particular, we encouraged discussion when we read the Scriptures together after our evening meal.[52] We wanted Jane and Paul to think through life issues in our home before being exposed to them from unbelieving outsiders. This also meant that we couldn't justify a number of longstanding Christian habits. We had to concede that the Bible says nothing about wearing dresses in church meetings or kids sitting in the same pew as their parents! But it says a lot about being rightly related to God through Jesus, and by his grace, our kids came to know him.

Moving specifically to church activities, pastors should encourage questions, too. Paul tells Timothy, effectively the pastor in Ephesus (cf. 1 Tim 1:3), to "set the believers an example in speech, in conduct, in love, in faith, in purity" (1 Tim 4:12b). While questioning isn't spelled out here, a few verses later Paul writes, "Keep a close watch on yourself and on the teaching" (1 Tim 4:16a). This implies a constant "log" removal process on the part

---

52 Family meals are a great place to encourage healthy questioning. As Joe Nangle notes in "The Breaking of Bread (Luke 24)," *Sojourners* 25.6 (1996): 49, "It is in the enjoyable atmosphere of eating and drinking in community that dialogue best happens, new ideas find expression, and contradictory opinions are safely stated and received." A helpful (though secular) source on the importance of family meals is Miriam Weinstein's *The Surprising Power of Family Meals: How Eating Together Makes Us Smarter, Stronger, Healthier, and Happier* (Hanover, NH: Steerforth, 2005).

of a pastor. As he does this, he sets the example for others to do the same. Given the focus on Scriptural instruction in this passage (vs. 13), it has to mean always checking that what he says reflects biblical truth.

I tell people I teach in church and seminary settings not to believe me because I have a Ph.D., but only if they're convinced that my teaching is biblical. I also encourage questions so that we can work through issues as we go. My personal style aside, I'm not saying a pastor must take questions from the pulpit.[53] However, questions for the congregation could be printed in a bulletin (and be a basis for note-taking). They might include the following: Did the sermon come from a Bible passage? If so, did the sermon say what the Bible passage says? Did the sermon include a gospel presentation?[54] Did the sermon give me biblical principles to practice? Questions like these do at least two things. They keep a pastor focused since he has alerted the congregation to what really matters. And they teach people to think (and speak) about the issues that concern our questioning God, both in church and wider society.[55]

Turning to wider society, our last area of focus, we have a much broader scope. Here we find all of humanity, monotheist and otherwise. Good questions for people we meet will vary as much

---

53 I have seen this done well, though, at the end of a sermon at Grace Toronto Church in Canada.

54 By this I mean a presentation of the good news that Jesus died on the cross for our sins and rose again from the dead (with an encouragement to respond to *him*), not a call to accept a rather vague Jesus in an immediately visible (but probably short-lived) way.

55 Unfortunately, many pastors wouldn't dream of encouraging this kind of questioning. Yet each of us is accountable to the questioning God. So in the case of question-resistant pastors (and other leaders), one should look constantly (and prayerfully) for appropriate questions to pose. Such questions should be preceded by "log" removal, to avoid being seen as a threat, but they may lead to the sad conclusion one is wasting one's time with the individual(s) concerned. It would then be better to focus on different people, possibly in another location.

as they do. I have suggested some questions for Muslims, Jews, and
Christians. My concluding example concerns an engagement with
a young Iranian man on legalism. In 1999, I was one of several
African diplomats invited by the government to spend five weeks
in Iran. During my fascinating stay there, I noticed that buses were
segregated with men at the front and women at the back. So I asked
Mohammad Nabi, our official minder, what would happen if a
man caught a bus with his nine-year-old daughter, but she had to
sit with a bunch of strangers at the back. Mohammad Nabi's
response was simply an irritated, "Why are you asking these
questions?!" That's as far as I got on happenings in the bus, but his
answer suggests that I had other questions for him (which I did).[56]
In any event, before we left Iran, he said he would miss us, adding
with a look at me, "Especially you!" I got the distinct impression
he had appreciated my engaging him on things he took for granted,
even though it left him without answers at the time. My point is
that Mohammad Nabi is not alone. There are people like him in
many different traditions, each one needing engagement, for they
typically take refuge in the comfortably familiar as a way to dodge
the questioning God.

The remaining challenge, then, is to listen with care and to grasp
unique individuals' values and concerns. Asking them leading
questions, and also responding to theirs, will follow. Of course,
people often use questions of their own to escape encountering
God through Christ while justifying themselves. Newman points
out that these questions are often versions of "Why does a good
God allow evil and suffering" (Newman, 114)? There are no easy
answers, and Newman rightly insists we admit our perplexity (*Ibid*,
110).[57] But he goes on to suggest that we turn such questions
around to get beyond the attempt to avoid the questioning God:

56 In retrospect, I suspect if the girl were old enough to be veiled, she
would join the other (veiled) women at the back of the bus, strangers though
they would be.
57 He is not saying one should ignore standard apologetic answers to the
problem of evil, but rather avoid a "know-it-all" attitude in doing so.

"In other words, how do *they*, as atheists or agnostics or skeptics, explain the Holocaust, AIDS, or September 11" (Ibid, 118, my emphasis)? The goal is to have people confront the issues, find there are no facile solutions, and then deal with the particularities of coming to know the questioning God on his terms.

Finally, as questioning beings, there is no limit to what we might ask, but our questions must always be anchored in the questioning God's enduring concern to engage us.

Select Bibliography

"*Aafaq* Editor-in-Chief Omran Salman: Saudi Arabia Has Squandered Opportunity to Renew its Aging Political System," *MEMRI Special Dispatch No. 1988*, July 17, 2008, http://memri.org/bin/articles.cgi?Page=archives&Area=sd&ID=SP198808 (accessed April 20, 2011).

Abdo, Geneive. *No God But God: Egypt and the Triumph of Islam*. Oxford: Oxford University Press, 2000.

_____. "A More Islamic Islam," *The Washington Post*, March 17, 2007, http://www.washingtonpost.com/wp-dyn/content/article/2007/03/16/AR2007031601941_pf.html (accessed April 21, 2011).

Al-Ghazali, Abu Hamid Muhammad Ibn Muhammad al-Tusi. *The Incoherence of the Philosophers: A parallel English-Arabic text*. Translated, introduced, and annotated by Michael E. Marmura. Provo, UT: Brigham Young University Press, 1997.

"Al-Jazeera TV Debate on Secularism, Islamism in Arab World Deteriorates Into Exchange of Insults," *The Middle East Media Research Institute* (MEMRI) *Special Dispatch No. 1767*, November 16, 2007, http://memri.org/bin/articles.cgi?Page=archives&Area=sd&ID=SP176707 (accessed April 20, 2011).

An-Na'im, Abdullahi Ahmed. "The Islamic Law of Apostasy and its Modern Applicability: A Case from the Sudan." *Religion* 16 (1986): 197-224.

Baig, Mirza Yawar, "The Ummah (Muslim Community) is Hemorrhaging," *The Wisdom Fund*, January 26, 2007, http://www.twf.org/News/Y2007/0126-Baig.html (accessed April 20, 2011).

Banerjee, Neela. "Conservative Rabbis to Vote on Resolution Criticizing Pope's Revision of Prayer," *New York Times*, February 9, 2008, http://www.nytimes.com/2008/02/09/

us/09prayer.html?_r=1&ei=5087&em=&en=4c84e237072
a6 (accessed June 3, 2011).

Brickner, David. "New Opinion Poll on What Israelis Think
    About Jesus," *Jews for Jesus*, May 15, 2008,
    http://jewsforjesus.org/publications/realtime/59/01 (ac-
    cessed June 3, 2011).

_____. "A Note from David Brickner: Why Don't the
    Rabbis Believe in Jesus?" *Jews for Jesus*, January 15, 2010,
    http://www.jewsforjesus.org/publications/realtime/79/01
    ?rt79 (accessed June 6, 2011).

Bridges, Jerry. *The Discipline of Grace: God's Role and Our Role in the
    Pursuit of Holiness.* Colorado Springs: NavPress, 2006.

Brooks, David. "A Loud and Promised Land," *New York Times*,
    April 16, 2009, http://www.nytimes.com/2009/04/
    17/opinion/17brooks.html (accessed June 1, 2011).

_____. "The Tel Aviv Cluster," *The New York Times*, January
    11, 2010, http://www.nytimes.com/2010/01/12/
    opinion/12brooks.html (accessed May 25, 2011).

_____. "The Arduous Community," *The New York Times*,
    December 20, 2010, http://www.nytimes.com/
    2010/12/21/opinion/21brooks.html (accessed May 26,
    2011).

Brown, Michael L. *Answering Jewish Objections to Jesus.* Grand
    Rapids: Baker, 2000.

Bukhari, Sahih 001.001.003, tr. M. Muhsin Khan,
    http://www.usc.edu/schools/college/crcc/engagement/
    resources/texts/muslim/hadith/bukhari/001.sbt.html
    (accessed August 2, 2011).

Carson, D.A. "Matthew." In *The Expositor's Bible Commentary* vol.
    8, ed. Frank E. Gæbelein Grand Rapids: Regency
    Reference Library, 1984, 1–599.

Chapman, Colin. *Whose Promised Land? The Continuing Crisis over
    Israel and Palestine* Grand Rapids: Baker, 2002.

Christianson, Eric S. "Sacred Writings." In *Introduction to World
    Religions*, ed. Christopher Partridge. Minneapolis: Fortress,
    2005, 282–86.

Dickson, John. *A Spectator's Guide to World Religions: An Introduction to the Big Five.* Oxford: Lion Hudson, 2008.

Dinter, Paul E. *Beyond Naive Belief: The Bible and Adult Catholic Faith.* New York: Crossroad, 1994.

"Disgusting Support for Baruch Goldstein," *Jewlicious*, March 4, 2010, http://www.jewlicious.com/2010/03/disgusting-support-for-baruch-goldstein/ (accessed June 1, 2011).

"Egyptian Liberal Magdi Khalil: Muslim Representatives Are Subverting the International Human Rights System from Within," *MEMRI Special Dispatch No. 2459*, July 23, 2009, http://memri.org/bin/articles.cgi?Page=archives&Area=sd&ID=SP245909 (accessed April 29, 2011).

Ehrens, David. Reader Comment on "The Telegraph: Odds & ends from the staff of JTA," *JTA*, August 21, 2009, http://blogs.jta.org/telegraph/article/2009/08/21/1007386/huckabee-on-evangelicals-palestinian-state (accessed June 1, 2011).

Ellis, Marc H. *Judaism Does Not Equal Israel.* New York: The New Press, 2009.

"Former Saudi Shura Council member Ibrahim Al-Buleihi: The Arabs' Delusion of Their Own Perfection Makes It Impossible for Them to Benefit from Modern Culture," *MEMRI Special Dispatch No. 2880*, March 30, 2010, http://www.memri.org/report/en/0/0/0/0/0/254/4063.htm (accessed April 20, 2011).

Friedman, Thomas L. "People vs. Dinosaurs," *The New York Times*, June 8, 2008, http://www.nytimes.com/2008/06/08/opinion/08friedman.html?ei=5087&em=&en=d2eeef6 (accessed May 23, 2011).

Gilley, Gary E. *This Little Church Went to Market: The Church in the Age of Entertainment.* Webster, NY: Evangelical Press, 2005.

Gopnik, Alison. "Your Baby Is Smarter Than You Think," *The New York Times*, August 15, 2009, http://www.nytimes.com/2009/08/16/opinion/16gopnik.html?_r=1&pagewanted=1 (accessed April 1, 2011).

Greenham, Ant. *Muslim Conversions to Christ: An Investigation of Palestinian Converts Living in the Holy Land.* EMS Dissertation

Series, ed. Richard L. Starcher. Pasadena: WCIU Press, 2004.

Gushee, David P. "What the Torture Debate Reveals about American Christianity." In *Religious Faith, Torture, and Our National Soul*, ed. David P. Gushee, Jillian Hickman Zimmer, and J. Drew Zimmer. Macon: Mercer University Press, 2010, 71–91.

Hart, David Bentley. *Atheist Delusions: The Christian Revolution and Its Fashionable Enemies*. New Haven: Yale University Press, 2009.

Hayes, Josh. "SBTS: Panel ponders 'Amusing Ourselves to Death,'" *Baptist Press*, March 8, 2011, http://www.bpnews.net/bpnews.asp?ID=34789 (accessed June 27, 2011).

Hellwig, Monika K. *Understanding Catholicism*. 2d ed. New York: Paulist Press, 2002.

Hourani, Albert. *A History of the Arab Peoples*. New York: MJF Books, 1991.

Houssney, Georges. *Engaging Islam*. Boulder: Treeline Publishing, 2010.

Huff, Toby E. *The Rise of Early Modern Science: Islam, China, and the West*. 2d ed. Cambridge: Cambridge University Press, 2003.

"Iraq: The Betrayal of the Christians." *Barnabas Aid* (November/December 2007): 6–10.

Jaki, Stanley L. *Science and Creation: From Eternal Cycles to an Oscillating Universe*. Rev. ed. Edinburgh: Scottish Academic Press, 1986.

Jenkins, Philip. *The New Faces of Christianity: Believing the Bible in the Global South*. Oxford: Oxford University Press, 2006.

_____. *The Lost History of Christianity: The Thousand-Year Golden Age of the Church in the Middle East, Africa, and Asia—and How It Died*. New York: HarperOne, 2008.

Kennedy, John W. "Healing ORU," *Christianity Today*, September 3, 2008, http://www.christianitytoday.com/ct/2008/september/8.76.html?start=1 (accessed June 29, 2011).

Lewis, Charles. "Wafergate: Purportedly Pocketed Host Embroils Harper in Religious 'Scandal'," *National Post*, July 8, 2009, http://network.nationalpost.com/np/blogs/holy-post/archive/2009/07/08/wafergate-purportedly-pocketed-host-embroils-harper-in-religious-scandal.aspx (accessed June 13, 2011).

Mangalwadi, Vishal. *Truth and Transformation: A Manifesto for Ailing Nations.* Seattle: YWAM Publishing, 2009.

Marsh, Charles. *Wayward Christian Soldiers: Freeing the Gospel from Political Captivity.* Oxford: Oxford University Press, 2007.

Massie, Robert Kinloch. *Loosing the Bonds: The United States and South Africa in the Apartheid Years.* New York: Nan A. Talese, 1997.

McBrien, Richard P. *Catholicism.* New ed. San Francisco: HarperSanFrancisco, 1994.

McGrath, Alister E. *Christian Theology: An Introduction.* 4th ed. Malden, MA: Blackwell Publishers, 2007.

Middelmann, Udo. *Christianity versus Fatalistic Religions in the War Against Poverty.* Colorado Springs: Paternoster, 2007.

Mirsky, Yehudah. "Beyond 'Religious' and 'Secular'," *Jewish Ideas Daily*, May 11, 2011, http://www.jewishideasdaily.com/content/module/2011/5/11/main-feature/1/beyond-religious-and-secular (accessed May 25, 2011).

Muller, Roland. *Tools for Muslim Evangelism.* Belleville, Canada: Essence, 2000.

Nangle, Joe. "The Breaking of Bread (Luke 24)." *Sojourners* 25.6 (1996): 49.

Neuman, Abraham A. *The Jews in Spain: Their Social, Political and Cultural Life During the Middle Ages.* Philadelphia: The Jewish Publication Society of America, 1948.

Newman, Randy. *Questioning Evangelism: Engaging People's Hearts the Way Jesus Did.* Grand Rapids: Kregel, 2004.

Nisbett, Richard E. *The Geography of Thought: How Asians and Westerners Think Differently and Why.* New York: The Free Press, 2003.

Noll, Mark A. *The New Shape of World Christianity: How American Experience Reflects Global Faith.* Downers Grove: InterVarsity Press, 2009.

Philpott, Kent. *Are You Really Born Again? Understanding True and False Conversion,* 2d ed. Webster, NY: Evangelical Press, 2005.

Piper, John. *Think: The Life of the Mind and the Love of God.* Wheaton: Crossway, 2010.

Postman, Neil. *Amusing Ourselves to Death: Public Discourse in the Age of Show Business.* New York: Penguin, 1986.

Reilly, Robert R. *The Closing of the Muslim Mind: How Intellectual Suicide Created the Modern Islamist Crisis.* Wilmington, DE: ISI Books, 2010.

Ruden, Sarah. *Paul Among the People: The Apostle Reinterpreted and Reimagined in His Own Time.* New York: Pantheon, 2010.

"Saudi Intellectual: Western Civilization Has Liberated Mankind," *MEMRI Special Dispatch No. 2332,* April 29, 2009, http://memri.org/bin/articles.cgi?Page=archives&Area=sd&ID=SP233209 (accessed April 20, 2011).

"Second Iraqi Christian Murdered in Two Weeks," *Barnabas Aid,* June 8, 2011, http://barnabasfund.org/US/News/News-analysis/Second-Iraqi-Christian-murdered-in-two-weeks.html (accessed June 28, 2011).

Shah, Timothy Samuel. "For the Sake of Conscience: Some Evangelical Views of the State." In *Church, State, and Citizen: Christian Approaches to Political Engagement,* ed. Sandra F. Joireman. Oxford: Oxford University Press, 2009, 113–43.

Strode, Tom (comp.), "U.N. Body Finally Shuns 'Defamation' Concept," *Baptist Press,* March 25, 2011, http://www.bpnews.net/bpnews.asp?ID=34925 (accessed April 29, 2011).

"Study: Israeli Jews also blame Israel for conflict," *JTA,* May 7, 2009, http://jta.org/news/article-print/2009/05/07/1005003/study-israeli-jews-more-critical-of-con (accessed June 1, 2011).

Teibel, Amy. "Ultra-Orthodox Seek Boycott of their own Web Sites," *Worldwide Religious News*, January 26, 2010, http://wwrn.org/articles/32524/ (accessed May 25, 2011).

Thubron, Colin. *Journey into Cyprus*. New York: The Atlantic Monthly Press, 1975.

Torczyner, Harry. "The Riddle in the Bible." *Hebrew Union College Annual* I (1924): 125–49.

"Ultra-Orthodox Jews in Mass Protest over School Ruling," *BBC*, June 17, 2010, http://www.bbc.co.uk/news/10338900 (accessed May 25, 2011).

Vu, Michelle A. "Egyptian President's Visit Magnifies Christian, Muslim Tension," *The Christian Post*, August 18, 2009, http://www.christianpost.com/article/20090818/egypt-president-s-visit-magnifies-christian-muslim-problem/page2.html (accessed May 2, 2011).

Weinstein, Miriam. *The Surprising Power of Family Meals: How Eating Together Makes Us Smarter, Stronger, Healthier, and Happier*. Hanover, NH: Steerforth, 2005.

Williams, D.H. *Retrieving the Tradition and Renewing Evangelicalism: A Primer for Suspicious Protestants*. Grand Rapids: Eerdmans, 1999.

Wilson, John. "The Apostle of the Golden Age," *Christianity Today*, September 22, 2010, http://www.christianitytoday.com/ct/2010/september/26.44.html?start=2 (accessed June 17, 2011).

Witherup, Ronald D. *Conversion in the New Testament*. Zacchaeus Studies: New Testament, ed. Mary Ann Getty. Collegeville, MN: Liturgical Press, 1994.

Topics and Persons Index

Scripture Index

Also in the
Areopagus Critical Christian Issues Series

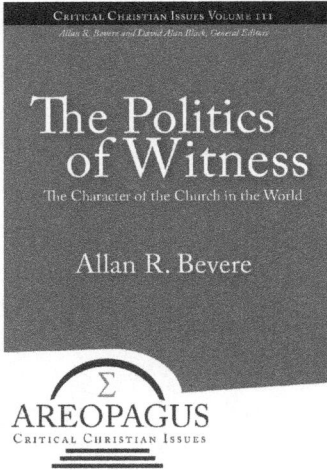

Allan Bevere, an ecclesial theologian, combines in this book a wonderful "church as politics" with gospel in a wise, warm and challenging manner.

— Scot McKnight

I believe the thrust and heart of this book are needed and crucial for the faith, life and witness of the church today. It is short, concise and affordable, one of those books one may want to work on, and good for reference.

— Ted M. Gossard

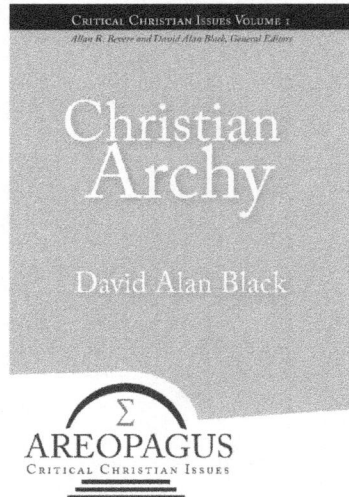

More from Energion Publications

Personal Study

The Jesus Paradigm	$17.99
Finding My Way in Christianity	$16.99
When People Speak for God	$17.99
Holy Smoke, Unholy Fire	$14.99
Not Ashamed of the Gospel	$12.99
Evidence for the Bible	$16.99
Christianity and Secularism	$16.99
What's In A Version?	$12.99
Christian Archy	$9.99
Ultimate Allegiance	$9.99
The Politics of Witness	$9.99

Christian Living

Daily Devotions of Ordinary People – Extraordinary God	$19.99
Directed Paths	$7.99
Grief: Finding the Candle of Light	$8.99
I Want to Pray	$7.99
Soup Kitchen for the Soul	$12.99

Bible Study

Learning and Living Scripture	$12.99
To the Hebrews: A Participatory Study Guide	$9.99
Revelation: A Participatory Study Guide	$9.99
The Gospel According to St. Luke: A Participatory Study Guide	$8.99
Philippians: A Participatory Study Guide	$9.99
Ephesians: A Participatory Study Guide	$9.99
Identifying Your Gifts and Service: Small Group Edition	$12.99
The Character of Our Discontent	$12.99
Why Four Gospels?	$11.99

Theology

The Church Under the Cross	$11.99
God's Desire for the Nations	$18.99
Out of This World: An Assessment of Christian Community	$24.99
From Inspiration to Understanding	$24.99

Generous Quantity Discounts Available
Energion Publications
P.O. Box 841 - Gonzalez, FL 32560
Website: http://energionpubs.com
Phone: (850) 525-3916

Ant Greenham was educated in South Africa and the United States. He has a Ph.D. in missions, with a focus on Islamic studies. Dr. Greenham has taught at Southeastern Baptist Theological Seminary since 2001, where he is Assistant Professor of Missions and Islamic Studies. Before that, he was employed by the South African Department of Foreign Affairs and during the 1980s and 1990s served in Tel Aviv and then in Amman, where he opened the first South African Embassy.

The *Areopagus Critical Christian Issues* series examines important issues in understanding Christian beliefs and developing sound Christian practice. Each booklet is short — less than 80 pages in length — and provides an academically sound and biblically rooted examination of a particular question about doctrine or practice or an area of basic Christian belief. It is jointly edited by Dr. Allan R. Bevere and Dr. David Alan Black.